# Managing Transnationalism in Northern Europe

## Westview Replica Editions

This book is a Westview Replica Edition. The concept of Replica Editions is a response to the crisis in academic and informational publishing. Library budgets for books have been severely curtailed; economic pressures on the university presses and the few private publishing companies primarily interested in scholarly manuscripts have severely limited the capacity of the industry to properly serve the academic and research communities. Many manuscripts dealing with important subjects, often representing the highest level of scholarship, are today not economically viable publishing projects. Or, if they are accepted for publication, they are often subject to lead times ranging from one to three years. Scholars are understandably frustrated when they realize that their first-class research cannot be published within a reasonable time frame, if at all.

Westview Replica Editions seem to us one feasible and practical solution to the crisis. The concept is simple. We accept a manuscript in camera-ready form and move it immediately into the production process. The responsibility for textual and copy editing lies with the author or sponsoring organization. If necessary we will advise the author on proper preparation of footnotes and bibliography. The manuscript is acceptable as typed for a thesis or dissertation or prepared in any other clearly organized and readable way, though we prefer it typed according to our specifications. The end result is a book produced by lithography and bound in hard covers. Edition sizes range from 300 to 600 copies. We will include among Westview Replica Editions only works of outstanding scholarly quality or of great informational value and we will exercise our usual editorial standards and quality control.

# Managing Transnationalism in Northern Europe

Bengt Sundelius

How can political leaders best control the effects of transnational links on their societies, maintaining the prosperity brought by such ties while minimizing their unstabilizing effects? The answer, according to some observers, rests in collective management through joint policy-making processes. This work explores the strategy used in Scandinavian countries for collectively coping with transnationalism. Although focusing on a unique case, it is highly relevant to broader international efforts at policy coordination and joint problem solving.

The author first analyzes the extent of Nordic transnational ties and identifies the principles involved in collective management. He then outlines the means, scope, and frequency of regional contacts among political leaders and bureaucrats and analyzes the norms and dynamics of joint policymaking to determine what roles the various principals play in the collective management effort. Policy results are reviewed in order to evaluate the relative success of Nordic methods, and comparisons are made between issue areas and degrees of salience to reveal the types of issues most effectively treated by the Nordic strategy.

Bengt Sundelius, a native of Sweden, is assistant professor of international studies at Bradley University. Dr. Sundelius has served as a participant observer on the Nordic Council and Council of Ministers.

# Managing
# Transnationalism
# in Northern Europe

## Bengt Sundelius

Westview Press / Boulder, Colorado

48299

*A Westview Replica Edition*

Copyright © 1978 by Westview Press, Inc.

Published in 1978 in the United States of America by
    Westview Press, Inc.
    5500 Central Avenue
    Boulder, Colorado 80301
    Frederick A. Praeger, Publisher

Library of Congress Catalog Card Number: 78-59862
ISBN: 0-89158-282-7

Printed and bound in the United States of America

# Contents

# List of Figures

# List of Tables

# Acknowledgments

This study has benefitted from the assistance, advice, and criticism given me in the Nordic countries. Numerous officials and political leaders have provided me with invaluable help in the form of information, materials, and personal views, on many aspects of Nordic interactions. None is mentioned and none is forgotten. Furthermore, the Secretariats of the Nordic Council and Council of Ministers in Stockholm, Oslo, and Copenhagen helped me gain access to materials, individuals, and meetings, which without this assistance would have been beyond my reach. In addition, I am grateful for helpful comments by several Scandinavian scholars, including Ake Landqvist, Martin Saeter, Karl-Einar Stalvant, and Claes Wiklund.

Research for the work was partially funded by the Graduate School of International Studies, University of Denver, and the Board for Research and Creative Production, Bradley University. I am indebted to both institutions for their generous financial support. I am also grateful for the encouragement and intellectual stimulation provided throughout the project by John P. de Gara, Fred A. Sondermann, and Edward T. Rowe.

Portions of chapter three previously appeared in my "Trans-Governmental Interactions in the Nordic Region", Cooperation and Conflict, Vol. 12, No. 2 (1977), 63-86 and I acknowledge the permission given me by the editor to use these materials here. Finally, I want to thank those who have helped in the preparation of the manuscript; Charles Miles, Julie O'Bradovich, and Jeanne Ulrich.

# Managing
# Transnationalism
# in Northern Europe

# 1. The Challenge of Transnationalism

During the last ten years considerable attention has been given to the phenomena of transnational relations. It has been commonly pointed out that today many nations of the world are linked by intensive nongovernmental ties covering many sectors of society. Empirical studies of trade flows, investments, business collaboration, migration, activities of interest groups, political parties, terrorist organizations, churches, foundations, and banks have all been presented recently. Some analysts have even suggested a need for a new paradigm of "world politics" to replace the more traditional model of interstate relations. [1]

The concept of interdependence has frequently been used to help describe contemporary international relations. [2] One assumption often made by scholars using this term has been that the existence of transnational flows linking distinct political entities in some way make these units dependent on each other for their continued survival. The distinction has also been made between sensitivity and vulnerability interdependence, where the latter infers a societal need to maintain such transnational links. Sensitivity interdependence simply refers to the notion that developments in one society are easily transferred or diffused into another unit through their common transnational links. [3] This line of reasoning would then suggest that the existence of transnationalism has certain effects on the participating societies. Not only are they sensitive to events or developments outside their borders but possibly they could not even continue to function without these links. Drastic interruptions or disturbances in their transnational activity would possibly result in damaging consequences for the society.

1

Another feature common to many advanced industrial nations is the increasing role of government in society. The political authorities are expected to provide numerous services to their constituents. The most crucial function to be performed is to ensure a stable, healthy economy benefiting the public. No government is anxious to face an election at a time of economic hardship or instability. Often, economic dissatisfaction is manifested by declining political support for the elites in government positions. As a means of protection against possible future political losses, the political authorities are interested in maintaining a stable, prosperous, and harmonious society. Because of this concern with being able to control the domestic environment, governments have also come to see a need for controlling their external setting. It is recognized that international developments are transmitted into the domestic arena and indirectly have an influence on the political status of the government. So, many governments are anxious to influence their external environment not mainly from a desire to change global structures per se but to protect their domestic support. As they are held responsible by their voters for domestic developments, they need to make sure they can predict and steer societal change.

In summarizing our argument so far, we note three inter-related features: the existence of transnational links which transmit societal change, the reliance on transnational activities for societal prosperity, and the desire of political elites to control their societies to remain in authority. We can now see that the growth of transnationalism presents a dilemma for the political authorities. On the one hand, they feel they need these links to maintain domestic affluence. On the other hand they fear the effects of these forces as they can undermine the societal management effort pursued. If it was possible, the most effective way of maintaining absolute control of society, would be to completely insulate it from its environment. However, as this option in the West is regarded as too costly in terms of economic prosperity and individual freedoms, the political leaders are left with the alternative of reducing the unstabilizing impacts of international factors.

It is here the issue of being able to cope with transnationalism arises. How can governments best, short of cutting off international links, maintain effective control of the effects of these forces on their societies? According to several observers, the answer rests in the capacity to collectively manage transnationalism.[4] Through collaboration with other governments facing identical dilemmas, the political authorities should be able to successfully minimize the undesired effects and maximize the beneficial aspects of transnationalism. To achieve this objective, participating governments must learn to coordinate their policies in a mutually satisfactory manner. Government policy cannot merely be determined by domestic considerations. Instead, a constant awareness must be maintained of how decisions will affect neighboring societies as well. If all governments followed this guideline, they would cope far more successfully with the domestic effects of transnationalism.

Obviously, few political regimes are willing to accept the restraints necessary to completely avoid undesirable outcomes. If they did, their effective political authority would in fact be surrendered to another government or to a supra-national decision-making body. Realistically, governments are aiming for solutions where policy coordination is achieved with a minimum of restraint on the ability to reach unilateral domestic goals. In other words, governments are eager to work collectively to reduce the undesired external impacts on their societies as long as this collaboration does not seriously hamper their own domestic management efforts. A fine point must be found between the acceptable limits to governmental independence and the minimum amount of effective policy coordination.

We can express this dilemma graphically as an inverse relationship between the variables of policy effectiveness and governmental autonomy. As the control of external disturbances (policy effectiveness) improves, the freedom to pursue unilateral domestic objectives (governmental autonomy) is reduced. Hopefully, an optimal solution can be found, as indicated in point $xy$, where governmental autonomy is minimally reduced while policy is still effective. It would be an interesting research task to establish the empirical

3

THE DILEMMA OF COPING WITH TRANSNATIONALISM

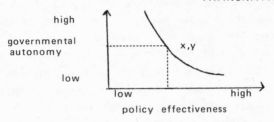

relationship between the two variables, be able to indicate how quickly a change in one variable induces changes in the other, and at what point an optimal balance between the two targets is achieved.   In order to comprehend the dilemma facing governments challenged by transnationalism and be able to recommend solutions, we need to understand the relationship between these two crucial variables.

Several analysts have suggested the usefulness of governmental elite networks, transgovernmental relations and multi-bureaucratic decision-processes as techniques of promoting policy coordination in the face of insistence on governmental autonomy.[5]   The national leadership, politicians, and bureaucrats, would need to engage in continuous interactions across a wide field of policy areas.   Such consultations would sensitize leaders to the needs and objectives of each other, help clear up misunderstandings of perception or belief, provide opportunities to consider alternative actions, make possible the exclusion of certain options, and possibly even facilitate agreements on a single course of action.   This way unintentional and unnecessary disturbances on neighboring societies caused by unilateral governmental decisions could be avoided.   This form of policy coordination is far less effective than the optimal management technique discussed above but it leaves each government fairly free to pursue its own particular goals within the broad limits set by collective understandings.

## Previous Research

Much of the literature on transnationalism deals with the American situation and the American need for management techniques.   For example, trans-Atlantic, trilateral, and U.S.-

Canadian relations have been extensively examined within this perspective.[6] These studies have pioneered the field and improved our understanding of the dynamics of transnationalism as well as our ability to comprehend what possible management techniques are available. The major shortcoming in relying so heavily on the American experience is that much of the theoretical conceptualization in the field is colored by the rather unique American situation. In many respects, the U.S. is an atypical case, facing tremendous opportunities and responsibilities not shared by other nations. Due to its giant size, active involvement in global affairs, special military status, and complex domestic structure, lessons learned in this case are not easily transferable to other actors in world affairs. If we were to concentrate too much of our research on this, unquestionably important as well as fascinating case, we would no doubt only uncover a part of the reality of transnationalism and its impact on governments. We need to test the findings from the American case in different settings where the unique American characteristics are not present.

The EC has provided another fertile ground for studies of the management of transnationalism. Several authors have pointed to the elaborate techniques adopted to solve transnational issues and for improving policy coordination among the members.[7] The research on the EC has generated many interesting findings and helped sharpen our awareness of what management techniques are tolerable to governments as well as what restrictions these place on a collective management effort. However, the formal European commitment to supranationalsim and eventual political union places this case apart. The basic value orientation of European integration can affect the techniques used, the options considered and the solutions adopted. Conslusions drawn within the EC framework might not be applicable in other areas, where the ultimate goal is not union but simply the successful management of transnationalism. So, it seems, the traditional research focus on the U.S. and the EC cases needs to be widened to include other areas. If so, we can hope to broaden the empirical base for our observations, refine previous findings and possibly even discover some different strategies for coping with transnationalism.

An exploration of the North European experiences of collective management of transnationalism can serve as a valuable complement to the other studies discussed. Not only can this region be viewed as a distinct transnational community, but the governments of Denmark, Finland, Iceland, Norway, and Sweden have developed sophisticated management techniques aimed at maintaining the political control of these societies. Here the objective is simply to cope with rapidly changing domestic and external environments. No ambitions about creating a regional political unit seem to influence the management process. Instead, the emphasis is on intimate collaboration within the framework of voluntarism and supreme national authority. At the same time, the Nordic countries are perhaps more typical of most advanced industrial societies. Their roles in world affairs are rather limited, their relatively small sizes make them easily penetrated by external developments, and economic aspirations tend to dominate over national security concerns. Hopefully, findings from this limited empirical setting can prove theoretically interesting to analysts of transnationalism as these would supplement experiences drawn from other areas.

So far, few scholars have explored North European relations within this perspective of coping with transnationalism. Instead, several studies of Nordic cooperation and integration have been made. Although the questions addressed in those works differ somewhat from the concerns here, many valuable insights into the dynamics of governmental collaboration in the region have been offered. In the present research effort we can draw on those observations, if we disregard the orientation toward integration or political union evident in much of the literature. Rather than evaluating the success/failure of integration or predicting the future course of cooperation, we concern ourselves with how the political authorities come to grips with the challenges of transnationalism and what techniques they use to cope with these forces.

The first clearly analytical study of Nordic cooperation was provided by Amitai Etzioni in 1965. This American sociologist

6

included the Nordic area as one of his four cases in a comparative study of political unification.[8] Many American observers still regard Etzioni's essay as the final word on the subject. There is no doubt that he presented many perceptive, insightful, and theoretically interesting conclusions on the Nordic process of cooperation. The major weakness of his work is the very limited empirical base for his conclusions. Etzioni was influenced by the unsuccessful efforts during the 1950's to create a Nordic Economic Market and saw much cooperation in light of that drawn out, uninspiring experience. The Nordic cooperation effort then seemed particularly hopeless when compared with the quicker and more dramatic expansion of European integration during the same period. In addition, Etzioni's work was hampered by a certain unfamiliarity with the Nordic region, a need to rely exclusively on secondary sources, an overemphasis on the formal aspects of cooperation, and a basic misunderstanding of the purpose and ambitions of Nordic cooperation. Still, this work must be seen as one of the most important studies of Nordic cooperation to date. This is the case due both to the great international circulation it had and because of the many theoretically interesting views it offered.

A second analytical study of great theoretical interest appeared two years after Etzioni volume. In 1967, the Swedish political scientist, Nils Andren, published a significant article on Nordic cooperation, which aimed at presenting a conceptual framework for future empirical studies.[9] Andren has been one of the main scholars to encourage more research on Nordic integration. He early recognized the great theoretical contribution such studies could make to the field of international relations. This article by Andren is especially valuable as it combines a fundamental understanding of the empirical reality of the Nordic relations with a keen concern for the analytical and theoretical aspects of this process. As such, one could expect that the framework suggested would have generated empirical studies of theoretical interest to outsiders. One reason why this has not happened is the operational difficulites with the proposed framework. Integration is vaguely defined in terms of increased interdependence, which in turn requires further specification before it can be used empirically. Unfortunately, the author does not solve any of the operational tasks but mainly outlines what areas could be studied if his framework were adopted. Thus, the article primarily provides an exploratory discussion of the field and includes numerous observations and ideas.

One of the most important thoughts presented by Andren is the "cobweb theory" of Nordic integration. This notion has had a great impact on both theorists and practitioners of cooperation in the region. The idea is that the many weak, sectorial Nordic ties in multiple areas together make up a strong cobweb of interdependencies that would be fairly difficult to break. The main weakness with this theory is that it ignores the question whether there is any conscious weaving of these webs, or if in fact the process of increased interdependence is unintentional.[10] Together with the Etzioni piece, the Andren essay is theoretically the most interesting and stimulating work published so far. The Andren contribution is especially valuable due to his intimate empirical knowledge of the Nordic process. In contrast to many foreign observers, Andren can base his theoretical conclusions on a firsthand and detailed knowledge of the regional activities.

A major empirical study of Nordic cooperation was also published in 1967.[11] This volume by Stanley Anderson on the Nordic Council deals exclusively with the institutional aspects of the cooperation process. Within that limited perspective, the analysis is comprehensive and rich with several valuable findings. Unfortunately, much of the structure described by Anderson has now changed considerably, which has made the book outdated in many respects. In addition, the author maintains a very formalistic, institutional view of political integration, which is not well suited for the Nordic experience. However, on the whole, this study provides a valuable empirical analysis of many important features of the cooperation process.

An important essay on the subject of Nordic cooperation is a 1974 article by Nils Orvik.[12] This scholar has written several articles on Nordic cooperation in which he has emphasized the role of external forces and the need to view Nordic cooperation in a foreign policy perspective.[13] In his latest article, Orvik presents an alternative framework to the Andren model discussed above. He argues that Nordic cooperation can best be analyzed through historical case studies of situations, where the Nordic option was considered and where the result was either a joint solution or failure. Orvik rejects the notion of interdependence and the use of systems analysis as a tool for Nordic integration studies. He instead emphasizes the decision-making approach as more valuable to reach conclusions about the various background factors behind joint cooperative ventures. Nordic cooperation issues should be treated as other foreign policy decisions, where calculations of benefits and costs are crucial to the outcome.

The major weakness with the Orvik approach is the over-emphasis on the state as a unified actor in Nordic cooperation. In many respects, Nordic relations cannot be seen as one feature of traditional foreign policy-making, but are more like an extension of domestic policy formulation without central governmental control or coordination. Except for some issues of vital national political importance, incremental and uncoordinated decisions concerning the relations with the other Nordic countries are made continuously throughout the governmental administrations. If one only analyzed decisions made by the central cabinets regarding the most crucial issues, one would ignore a substantial part of the cooperation process. Thus, the Orvik approach could be quite useful in exploring the major political decisions made in the region during the last fifty years, but it would only inadequately assist in a more comprehensive analysis of the broad and flexible trans-governmental relations at work.

One of Orvik's disciples, Barbara Haskel, has used an approach very similar to that of Orvik in analyzing the negotiations to form a Scandinavian defense alliance in 1948-49, the prolonged effort to create a Nordic economic market during the 1950's, and the successful work of the Nordic parliamentary committee on communications.[14] She adopts a costing perspective, where she tries to detect how the major participants in the cooperation process view the situation, the available options, and the costs and benefits of each possible strategy. Her study shows successfully the linkage between the domestic environment, international developments, and the regional cooperation process. One sees how these three arenas for political activity are all included simultaneously in the calculations by the political decision-makers. As with the Orvik essays, Haskel overemphasizes the role of calculated, long-term decisions in Nordic cooperation. While this could be the dominant perspective in a few situations involving the top leaders in each country, the large mass of issues are not handled in this centralized, rational manner.

In 1977, Erik Solem presented a study of the role of the Nordic Council in regional cooperation.[15] Here the institutional structures for Nordic cooperation are extensively discussed. Essentially, one gets an updated version of the observations in the earlier Anderson book. Also, a review of the major policy achievements generated by the Nordic Council is presented. Unfortunately, the work offers little of theoretical interest as it fails to place the observations made within the perspective of the current literature in the field.

Two recent articles on transgovernmental relations in the area should be mentioned. Robert Dickerman has presented some perceptive comments on the dynamics of transgovernmental decision-making processes and has made relevant comparisons with other cases. [16] His essay generates many fruitful hypotheses worthy of more intensive study. Bengt Sundelius has in more detail explored the intensive network of transgovernmental interactions and analyzed what roles various participants play in the resulting collective policy-making process. [17] We shall in this work further elaborate on the findings presented in this earlier article.

Finally, it must be emphasized that a number of other books and articles on Nordic cooperation have been published during the last 20 years. As our purpose was not to review the available literature on Nordic cooperation , but to point to some studies of special interest to our present research focus, we shall not comment on these other works but simply refer to the excellent reviews offered elsewhere. [18] Instead, we shall now turn to the framework guiding the empirical presentation.

## Present Research Focus

As indicated earlier, the objective of this study is to analyze the management techniques devised to cope with the effects of transnationalism in Northern Europe. It is our hope that observations about this collective management process will prove valuable to analysts of other similar efforts. This way the Nordic study can contribute both to the comparative analysis of transnationalism and to the improved theoretical understanding of this feature of international relations.

There are three basic assumptions underlying this work. First, the existence of transnational links across the national borders in the region has a significant impact on the societies involved. They make for penetrated societies, where events and developments in one society affect the others, (sensitivity), and where the links are so well entrenched in each society that a break of the ties would make for serious societal disturbances (vulnerability). Secondly, the national political authorities in the region have ambitions to control social and economic change to promote prosperity and stability within their political jurisdictions. This means that the governments have a need to protect their societies from disturbing external impacts. At the same time, they want to facilitate those transnational activities, which help ensure continued social and economic prosperity. Thirdly, the governments in the region have recognized that the only successful way to minimize the undesired effects and simultaneously maximize the desirable results of transnationalism is to engage in collective policy coordination. This does not infer that the political elites will always choose a collective strategy over a unilateral policy. We only assume that the leaders recognize the superior effectiveness of collective techniques. Often, they will prefer unilateral action as various domestic and international factors may induce them to give priority to other political needs. Only within the limits set by the domestic and international environments can the political authorities work out mutually satisfying solutions at the regional level.

We define transnational relations, interactions, links or ties, as non-governmental activities transcending the boundaries of political entities. Transnationalism refers to the existence of such links, networks or activities across national borders. Empirical indices of transnationalism, or a transnational community, can be found at two levels: at the aggregate level one notes the flow of transactions and at the elite level one analyzes the activities of non-governmental elite groups. We also differentiate between different types of transnational communities depending on what societal aspect is being exchanged. A transnational trade community is indicated by the flow of goods. A transnational communications community is indicated by the flow of messages. A transnational migration community is indicated by the flow of people. A transnational business community is indicated by business collaboration across national borders. The existence of transnational interest groups is indicated by regional networks of interest groups. In all cases, we are interested not only in the regional activities but also if there is any marked difference between activities within the region and those with the international environment. If so, one can claim that the region constitutes a distinct community set apart from its international surroundings. By examining these empirical dimensions along these lines we shall be able to point to the existence of a unique Nordic transnational community.

In order to understand the Nordic process of collective management we need to explore several dimensions of governmental collaboration. The institutional framework for the cooperation effort must be examined. The

11

major participants in the process must be identified. The forms and means of interaction must be explored. The norms guiding decision-making must be reviewed. Finally, the dynamics of policy coordination must be analyzed in order to understand how collective solutions are arrived at. This way, we can learn how the Nordic political authorities reach collective policy coordination in many issue areas.

To evaluate the relative success of the Nordic management effort one needs to study the results of collaboration, i.e., the joint policy output. If we can point to an impressive number of joint policies covering a wide scope of areas, we can also say something about how effective the Nordic strategy has been. By comparing the results in different areas we can also determine where the Nordic effort has proved most or least successful. It is quite likely that this technique for coping with transnationalism will fare better in some issue areas than in others. If so, we have learned some valuable lessons for the future, as well as for other experiments in coping.

To summarize the preceding discussion we can now list the research questions addressed throughout this study.

1. Does the North European region constitute a transnational community?
2. What aspects of society are linked by transnational ties?
3. What effects do these transnational relations have on the governments' ability to control their societies?
4. How do the political authorities view the problems associated with transnationalism?
5. What techniques have been adopted to manage the effects of transnationalism?
6. What political actors are involved in the management effort?
7. How do these actors interact with each other?
8. What roles do the different actors play in the policy coordination process?
9. What institutional structures have been established to facilitate collective action.
10. How do these institutions function in terms of authority and policy-making roles?
11. What norms are adhered to by the participants in the joint decision-making process?
12. How are collective solutions resulting in joint policy arrived at?
13. How successful has the Nordic strategy been in terms of joint policy output?
14. How does the performance differ between policy areas?

15. Are policy issues of higher salience handled less successfully than policy issues of lower salience?
16. What can we tell the political elites in the Nordic region to help them improve on their present management techniques?
17. What conclusions from this case are relevant to other experiments in collective management?
18. How can we relate our findings to the theoretical literature on trans-nationalism and what can we contribute to this?

# 2. A Transnational Community

This chapter is devoted to empirically test our contention that the Nordic region constitutes a transnational community. Several indicators are used, such as trade, communication and migration flows, business collaboration, and activities of interest groups. We will show how the Nordic political leaders are facing intense transnational interactions in many sectors of society. Increasingly, the Nordic borders are penetrated by these activities even to the extent that the political control of each national unity is seriously weakened. As the societies have come to depend on these transnational ties for material well being, it is very difficult for the governments to cut them off in order to increase their control. Rather, efforts must be tried to cooperate with other political units facing similar situations to better manage the Nordic transnational community.

## Trade

Inter-Nordic trade has increased substantially during the last twenty years. In Table 2:1 we see that in 1972 the total volume of exports by the Nordic countries to the Nordic area was six times as large, in market prices, as in 1952. To be able to evaluate the significance of this increase in regional trade, we need to look at Nordic trade as a proportion of total trade for each country. It is possible that the growth of the volume of Nordic trade has been combined with an even greater expansion of trade with other areas. If so, the Nordic interactions would not indicate the development of an exclusive Nordic community but merely be part of a world-wide increase in the transfer of goods during the post-war era.

## TABLE 2:1

VOLUME OF NORDIC TRADE 1952-1972
(Million of U.S. dollars at market prices)

| Year | DENMARK | | FINLAND | | ICELAND | | NORWAY | | SWEDEN | |
|---|---|---|---|---|---|---|---|---|---|---|
| | Exp | Imp | Exp | Imp | Exp | Imp | Exp | Imp | Exp | Imp |
| 1952 | 107.9 | 147.2 | 57.6 | 87.3 | 7.4 | 8.6 | 99.1 | 167.6 | 1571.5 | 1728.6 |
| 1956 | 146.7 | 185.0 | 41.0 | 87.2 | 6.8 | 14.1 | 138.8 | 217.3 | 1941.1 | 2207.7 |
| 1960 | 234.0 | 275.2 | 91.6 | 150.2 | 12.4 | 21.2 | 185.3 | 310.9 | 2566.9 | 2876.1 |
| 1964 | 411.3 | 505.1 | 137.9 | 241.7 | 24.7 | 33.0 | 304.4 | 511.6 | 3670.9 | 3852.7 |
| 1968 | 650.3 | 711.4 | 276.6 | 318.2 | 15.0 | 35.7 | 474.1 | 749.9 | 4937.3 | 5121.7 |
| 1972 | 1113.0 | 1203.7 | 754.3 | 738.3 | 22.7 | 60.7 | 853.1 | 1251.4 | 8614.3 | 8023.8 |

Sources: Direction of International Trade, 1952-1972 (Washington: International Monetary Fund).
Yearbook of Nordic Statistics, 1962-1974 (Stockholm: Nordic Council).

TABLE 2:2

REGIONAL PREFERENCE OF TRADE BY THE NORDIC COUNTRIES 1952-1972
(Percentage of total trade)

| From | To | 1952 | 1956 | 1960 | 1964 | 1968 | 1972 |
|---|---|---|---|---|---|---|---|
| **Export:** | | | | | | | |
| Denmark | Nordic | 12.7 | 13.2 | 15.7 | 19.4 | 25.2 | 25.7 |
| | EEC | 25.2 | 31.0 | 27.7 | 27.7 | 23.3 | 22.6 |
| Finland | Nordic | 8.0 | 5.3 | 9.3 | 10.7 | 16.9 | 25.6 |
| | EEC | 23.5 | 23.1 | 28.0 | 30.6 | 24.6 | 20.9 |
| Iceland | Nordic | 18.8 | 10.8 | 18.9 | 22.3 | 18.2 | 11.9 |
| | EEC | 22.1 | 19.0 | 14.5 | 16.2 | 14.8 | 16.2 |
| Norway | Nordic | 17.5 | 18.0 | 21.0 | 23.6 | 24.5 | 26.0 |
| | EEC | 23.5 | 25.8 | 25.7 | 26.2 | 23.4 | 23.8 |
| Sweden | Nordic | 16.0 | 16.3 | 20.0 | 24.2 | 24.7 | 25.2 |
| | EEC | 29.6 | 34.0 | 31.6 | 31.6 | 27.1 | 25.8 |
| **Import:** | | | | | | | |
| Nordic | Denmark | 15.3 | 14.1 | 15.3 | 19.3 | 22.1 | 23.8 |
| EEC | | 34.1 | 36.0 | 39.3 | 32.6 | 32.7 | 33.5 |
| Nordic | Finland | 11.0 | 9.9 | 14.2 | 16.1 | 20.0 | 23.1 |
| EEC | | 32.0 | 25.1 | 33.9 | 29.8 | 26.3 | 27.5 |
| Nordic | Iceland | 15.4 | 15.6 | 24.1 | 25.2 | 25.8 | 26.0 |
| EEC | | 11.6 | 17.8 | 22.3 | 17.9 | 28.0 | 27.5 |
| Nordic | Norway | 19.2 | 18.0 | 21.3 | 25.8 | 27.7 | 28.6 |
| EEC | | 26.0 | 31.0 | 32.7 | 28.9 | 24.7 | 26.3 |
| Nordic | Sweden | 7.8 | 7.9 | 9.6 | 13.2 | 16.5 | 20.5 |
| EEC | | 35.0 | 40.1 | 40.1 | 37.4 | 34.3 | 33.4 |

Sources: Direction of International Trade, 1952-1972 (Washington, D.C.: International Monetary Fund).
Yearbook of Nordic Statistics, 1962-1974 (Stockholm: Nordic Council).

17

## TABLE 2:3

## INTENSITY OF NORDIC TRADE FLOWS 1952-1972[a]

| Year | From: To: | DENMARK Nordic | EEC | FINLAND Nordic | EEC | ICELAND Nordic | EEC | NORWAY Nordic | EEC | SWEDEN Nordic | EEC |
|---|---|---|---|---|---|---|---|---|---|---|---|
| 1952 | | 89 | 26 | 45 | 20 | 4.8 | 1.0 | 76 | 16 | 291 | 55 |
| 1956 | | 91 | 28 | 24 | 15 | 3.4 | 1.0 | 81 | 16 | 303 | 54 |
| 1960 | | 111 | 24 | 41 | 16 | 4.7 | 0.5 | 82 | 13 | 365 | 47 |
| 1964 | | 152 | 24 | 48 | 17 | 7.3 | 0.8 | 104 | 14 | 486 | 50 |
| 1968 | | 162 | 17 | 63 | 12 | 2.9 | 0.4 | 109 | 13 | 456 | 39 |
| 1972 | | 175 | 17 | 107 | 10 | 2.8 | 0.5 | 123 | 13 | 490 | 38 |

[a]The scores were derived by dividing the absolute volume of exports to a region by the GNP of that region. To avoid decimals, this ratio was multiplied by 10,000. The index controls for the varying size of the different target areas for Nordic exports and measures the intensity of transactions.

It is quite clear in Table 2:2 that the Nordic region has become more important as a market and as a source of imports for the Nordic countries during the time period studied. While in 1952 less than 15 percent of total exports went to the Nordic region, in 1972 over 25% did. We also see in the table that the EC decreased in importance during the 1960s and in 1972 accounted for 30 percent of the trade. On the whole, we find the Nordic countries have become less dependent on extra-regional trading partners and instead are more closely tied to each other.

It is interesting that the very small Nordic economies, as compared to the EC economy, absorb about one-fourth of Nordic trade. In 1972 the Nordic region consisted of a market of merely 22 million people and had a combined GNP of about 82,000 million dollars. These figures can be compared with the population of the EC of 188 million people and a GNP of 592,000 million dollars in 1972. If we control for this vast difference in size of the Nordic and EC economies, we find in Table 2:3 that the intensity of inter-Nordic trade is far higher than for transactions with the EC. Thus, the Nordic region stands apart as a distinct transnational trade community.

## Communications

While regional trade flows are indicative of a transnational economic community, the flow of messages is related to the need for communications among the societies. We will analyze both mail flows and the number of telephone calls exchanged as one can expect the telephone to be particularly important in this area of close language similarities. With improved telecommunications technology it is also possible that much of the message flow previously handled by mail today is exchanged by telephone.

Table 2:4 indicates that the volume of letters exchanged among the Nordic societies has more than doubled during the last twenty years. The growth of telephone messages has been even greater. If we disregard Iceland, we see that in 1972 more than ten times as many telephone calls were exchanged as in 1952. No doubt these changes in the volume of the messages sent during the period are indicative of a greatly increased flow of communications among the Nordic societies.

19

## TABLE 2:4

## VOLUME OF NORDIC COMMUNICATION FLOWS 1952-1972
### (Thousands of letters and thousands of minutes)

From Country to Nordic Region

| Year | DENMARK Mail | DENMARK Phone | FINLAND Mail | FINLAND Phone | ICELAND Mail | ICELAND Phone | NORWAY Mail | NORWAY Phone | SWEDEN Mail | SWEDEN Phone |
|---|---|---|---|---|---|---|---|---|---|---|
| 1952 | 8337.0 | 2616.0 | — | 1243.3 | — | — | 5879.8 | 1856.7 | 12278.8 | 4307.9 |
| 1956 | 9151.6 | 3368.6 | — | 1700.9 | — | — | 7063.8 | 2532.9 | 15285.8 | 6355.0 |
| 1960 | 10666.0 | 5689.8 | 8469.8[a] | 2153.4 | — | — | 8988.2 | 4184.5 | 15015.4 | 9447.8 |
| 1964 | 12969.4 | 11585.7 | 8624.2 | 3597.8 | 483.9[b] | 189.4[b] | 11206.4 | 7423.0 | 18980.8 | 38077.5 |
| 1968 | 14569.7 | 19168.0 | 14632.5[c] | 6987.4 | 529.7 | 120.0[c] | 10641.8 | 11711.1 | 22336.0 | 29042.9 |
| 1972 | 19470.6 | 27375.7 | 18027.3 | 13411.4 | 526.3 | 216.2 | 13032.6 | 21905.5 | 21611.0 | 52412.6 |

[a] 1961.
[b] 1967.
[c] 1969.

Source: Yearbooks of the National Postal and Telephone and Telegraph Services of Denmark, Finland, Iceland, Norway, and Sweden, 1952-1972.

TABLE 2:5

COMMUNICATION FLOWS FROM THE NORDIC COUNTRIES TO THE NORDIC AND EEC REGIONS 1952-1972
(Percentage of total foreign flows)

From:

| Year | DENMARK | | | | FINLAND | | | | ICELAND | | | |
|------|------|------|------|------|------|------|------|------|------|------|------|------|
| | Mail | | Phone | | Mail | | Phone | | Mail | | Phone | |
| To: | Nord | EEC | Nord | EEC | Nord | EEC | Nord | EEC | Nord | EEC | Nord | EEC |
| 1952 | 36.6 | 24.0 | 62.7 | 26.3 | — | — | 85.3 | 7.1 | — | — | — | — |
| 1956 | 34.1 | 25.5 | 78.7 | 30.4 | — | — | 83.6 | 7.5 | — | — | — | — |
| 1960 | 30.8 | 26.7 | 60.9 | 28.3 | 44.6[a] | 22.6[a] | 81.5 | 9.1 | — | — | — | — |
| 1964 | 32.2 | 24.8 | 61.3 | 28.0 | 38.0 | 21.4 | 82.3 | 8.0 | 31.4 | 21.2 | 53.9 | 12.6 |
| 1968 | 31.5 | 23.4 | 62.0 | 25.7 | 46.4[b] | 20.6[b] | 83.8 | 7.2 | 35.5[b] | 20.2[b] | 47.1[b] | 15.8[b] |
| 1972 | 34.1 | 23.7 | 55.7 | 28.3 | 43.1 | 30.0 | 83.3 | 7.6 | 33.0 | 18.7 | 46.5 | 13.4 |

From:

| Year | NORWAY | | | | SWEDEN | | | |
|------|------|------|------|------|------|------|------|------|
| | Mail | | Phone | | Mail | | Phone | |
| To: | Nord | EEC | Nord | EEC | Nord | EEC | Nord | EEC |
| 1952 | 32.9 | 20.9 | 83.7 | 8.0 | 35.9 | 14.2[c] | 83.0 | 10.8 |
| 1956 | 31.4 | 21.8 | 81.2 | 9.4 | 34.5 | 16.9[c] | 83.2 | 10.8 |
| 1960 | 32.4 | 24.3 | 80.9 | 9.5 | 27.5 | 17.0[c] | 81.9 | 10.9 |
| 1964 | 31.8 | 20.5 | 81.3 | 8.8 | 30.4 | 13.5[c] | 79.9 | 11.9 |
| 1968 | 31.5 | 18.9 | 76.3 | 12.1 | 28.4 | 12.8[c] | 79.5 | 12.2 |
| 1972 | 35.8 | 17.9 | 68.8 | 14.8 | 28.0 | 11.0[c] | 68.1 | 20.5 |

[a] 1961.
[b] 1969.
[c] West Germany only.

Source: Yearbooks of the National Postal and Telephone and Telegraph Services of Denmark, Finland, Iceland, Norway, and Sweden, 1952-1972.

As we expected, the telephone calls have come to dominate the Nordic exchanges, while the mail flows have stagnated somewhat. One could also argue that there is a qualitative difference between messages transmitted by personal contact on the telephone and by mail. While letters are often rather formal, distant forms of communication, telephone calls bring the messenger into direct contact with the receiver. Thus, the effects of a telephone communication could be considerably different from those of a letter. We will see in a later chapter how the extensive use of the telephone for consultation and decision-making among various governmental officials has important integrative effects for the joint policy-making process in the region. For now, we are interested in finding out if the Nordic communication flows are significantly more intensive than those with the external world.

We find in Table 2:5 that inter-Nordic mail accounts for approximately 30 percent of the total mail flow from the Nordic countries. The rate is fairly stable over time and only in Sweden can we note a marked proportional decline. The EC countries get about 20 percent of the total mail from all Nordic countries. This rate is also stable over time. Obviously, the Nordic region takes a proportionally larger share of the total foreign mail from the Nordic countries than any external region. The proportion of regional telephone calls to all foreign calls is even greater than the the proportion of regional mail flow to total foreign mail flow. In 1972 the Nordic region accounted for well over 50 percent of all transnational calls made in all countries except Iceland. Denmark has the strongest ties to the EC countries as about 30 percent of all her calls go to that group. However, many of those calls are border conversations between the southern Danish province and the north German area.

In Table 2:6 we have divided the volume of mail and telephone calls by the population sizes of the target areas. This allows us to see more clearly the disproportionally greater intensity of both mail flows and telephone calls sent to the Nordic area as compared to the EC countries. The figures indicate that the frequency of inter-Nordic messages per receiver is far higher than for exchanges with other societies. Thus, the Nordic region seems to constitute a distinct system of transnational communication networks.

## TABLE 2:6

## INTENSITY OF NORDIC COMMUNICATION FLOWS 1952-1972*

**DENMARK**

| Year To: From: | Mail Nord | Mail EEC | Phone Nord | Phone EEC |
|---|---|---|---|---|
| 1952 | 56 | 4 | 18 | 0.7 |
| 1956 | 60 | 4 | 22 | 0.8 |
| 1960 | 68 | 5 | 36 | 1.6 |
| 1964 | 81 | 6 | 72 | 3.7 |
| 1968 | 88 | 6 | 115 | 4.3 |
| 1972 | 115 | 7 | 172 | 7.4 |

**FINLAND**

| Year | Mail Nord | Mail EEC | Phone Nord | Phone EEC |
|---|---|---|---|---|
| 1952 | – | – | 8 | 0.05 |
| 1956 | – | – | 11 | 0.09 |
| 1960 | 54[a] | 3[a] | 14 | 0.14 |
| 1964 | 53 | 3 | 22 | 0.20 |
| 1968 | 87[b] | 4[b] | 42 | 0.32 |
| 1972 | 104 | 7 | 78 | 0.52 |

**ICELAND**

| Year | Mail Nord | Mail EEC | Phone Nord | Phone EEC |
|---|---|---|---|---|
| 1952 | – | – | – | – |
| 1956 | – | – | – | – |
| 1960 | – | – | – | – |
| 1964 | 2 | 0.2 | 1 | 0.02 |
| 1968 | 2[b] | 0.2[b] | 0.6[b] | 0.02[b] |
| 1972 | 2 | 0.2 | 1.1 | 0.03 |

**NORWAY**

| Year From: | Mail Nord | Mail EEC | Phone Nord | Phone EEC |
|---|---|---|---|---|
| 1952 | 37 | 2 | 12 | 0.1 |
| 1956 | 44 | 3 | 16 | 0.2 |
| 1960 | 54 | 4 | 25 | 0.3 |
| 1964 | 66 | 4 | 43 | 0.5 |
| 1968 | 60 | 3 | 83 | 1.3 |
| 1972 | 72 | 3 | 121 | 2.5 |

**SWEDEN**

| Year | Mail Nord | Mail EEC | Phone Nord | Phone EEC |
|---|---|---|---|---|
| 1952 | 103 | 10[c] | 36 | 0.5 |
| 1956 | 124 | 15[c] | 52 | 0.7 |
| 1960 | 117 | 17[c] | 74 | 0.9 |
| 1964 | 145 | 15[c] | 291 | 1.7 |
| 1968 | 164 | 17[c] | 214 | 2.9 |
| 1972 | 155 | 14[c] | 377 | 8.0 |

[a] 1961.
[b] 1969.
[c] West Germany only.

*The scores were derived by dividing the absolute volume of messages sent to a region by the population size of the region. To avoid decimals this ratio was multiplied by 100.

TABLE 2:7    VOLUME OF NORDIC MIGRATION 1951-1973[1]

| From/To | Denmark | Finland | Norway | Sweden | Total |
|---|---|---|---|---|---|
| Denmark | — | 5900[a] | 75000 | 75300 | 156200 |
| Finland | 9400[a] | — | 6000[b] | 329800 | 345200 |
| Norway | 77400 | 4600[b] | — | 54200 | 136200 |
| Sweden | 61800 | 139100 | 42400 | — | 243300 |
| Total | 148600 | 149600 | 123400 | 459300 | 880900 |

[1]Iceland is excluded.
[a]1951-1972
[b]1956-1973
Source:   Nordic Council:   Annual Record, 1975, C1 p. 90.

## Migration

Data on migration across national boudaries are valuable indicators
of a transnational labor community.  Generally, political authorities
restrict or control the entry of foreigners into society so as not to
adversely affect employment, wages, or political stability.  Since July
first, 1954, a common Nordic labor market has made it possible to
move freely across national borders in search of better living conditions.
We note in Table 2:7 that this labor market has mainly benefitted the
flow of Finnish workers into Swedish industry.  In fact, over one half
of all Nordic migration during  1951-1973 has taken place between
Finland and Sweden.

When analyzing the origins of immigrants and the destination of
Nordic emigrants, we find in Table 2:8 that the Nordic flows are proportionally the dominant for all countries in the region.  The regional
mobility seems to outweigh any transfers between the region and any
specific external areas but the proportions are  less impressive here than
for the communication data.

In order to get a view of the more long-range and stable transfers
across the national boundaries in the region, we will focus  on those
individuals who changed their citizenship.  It is particularly important
to know where new citizens originate, as these individuals most likely
will maintain life-long links with their former home countries.  If there
is a considerable influx of permanent Nordic settlers in a country, one
can assume that these groups will be interested in promoting closer ties
within the area.  Our observations will here focus on Sweden, which

24

## TABLE 2:8

## MIGRATION BETWEEN THE NORDIC COUNTRIES AND THE NORDIC AND EEC REGIONS 1952-1972

(Percentage of total foreign migration of country)

### From: DENMARK

| Year To: | DENMARK Nord | EEC | FINLAND Nord | EEC | ICELAND Nord | EEC | NORWAY Nord | EEC | SWEDEN Nord | EEC |
|---|---|---|---|---|---|---|---|---|---|---|
| 1952 | — | — | — | — | — | — | — | — | 54.7 | 10.5 |
| 1956 | — | — | — | — | — | — | — | — | 48.2 | 18.4 |
| 1960 | 33.6 | 12.7 | — | — | 31.6[a] | 5.9[a] | 53.0[a] | 9.6[a] | 50.7 | 17.3 |
| 1964 | 30.5 | 13.7 | — | — | 41.2[b] | 14.8[b] | 47.4 | 11.2 | 49.6[c] | 17.8 |
| 1968 | 21.6[d] | 12.1[d] | 77.7[e] | 4.1[e] | 50.9[c] | 6.0[c] | 37.9 | 14.1 | 49.4[c] | 14.5 |
| 1972 | 21.3[d] | 12.6[d] | 91.4[e] | 1.4[e] | 60.2 | 6.0 | 37.4 | 10.7 | 58.3 | 9.9 |

### To: DENMARK

| Year From: | DENMARK Nord | EEC | FINLAND Nord | EEC | ICELAND Nord | EEC | NORWAY Nord | EEC | SWEDEN Nord | EEC |
|---|---|---|---|---|---|---|---|---|---|---|
| 1952 | — | — | — | — | — | — | — | — | 55.4 | 29.4 |
| 1956 | — | — | — | — | — | — | — | — | 64.4 | 19.1 |
| 1960 | 38.6 | 13.3 | — | — | 33.6[a] | 16.3[a] | 44.2[a] | 12.6[a] | 66.1 | 12.9 |
| 1964 | 29.6 | 16.0 | — | — | 40.3[b] | 15.5[b] | 41.0 | 12.7 | 64.6[c] | 13.4 |
| 1968 | 23.5 | 13.3[d] | 40.4[e] | 5.9[e] | 39.8[c] | 15.4[c] | 39.5 | 10.8 | 67.5[c] | 5.2[c] |
| 1972 | 22.0 | 10.3[d] | 83.2[e] | 2.3[e] | 55.2 | 6.4 | 33.4 | 9.7 | 48.8 | 8.0 |

[a] 1961.  [b] 1963.  [c] 1969.  [d] 1971.  [e] 1970.

Sources: Yearbook of Nordic Statistics, 1962-1974 (Stockholm: Nordic Council).
Statistical Abstracts of Sweden, 1952-1960 (Stockholm: Norstedt, 1952-1960).

## TABLE 2:9

### FOREIGNERS RECEIVING SWEDISH CITIZENSHIP 1952-1970

| Origin: Year | N | Nordic % | EEC-Countries N | % | Great Britain N | % | East Europe N | % | USA N | % | World N | % |
|---|---|---|---|---|---|---|---|---|---|---|---|---|
| 1952 | 2729 | 43.6 | 583[a] | 9.3[a] | 36 | 0.6 | 2207 | 35.3 | 222 | 3.6 | 6253 | 100 |
| 1955 | 3719 | 34.8 | 1250[a] | 11.7[a] | 48 | 0.4 | 4068 | 38.1 | 183 | 1.7 | 10686 | 100 |
| 1958 | 4260 | 45.5 | 1674[a] | 17.9[a] | 41 | 0.4 | 2221 | 23.7 | 202 | 2.2 | 9359 | 100 |
| 1961 | 3667 | 47.3 | 2054 | 26.5 | 36 | 0.5 | 436 | 5.6 | 210 | 2.4 | 7745 | 100 |
| 1964 | 4010 | 40.8 | 1871 | 19.1 | 45 | 0.5 | 2369 | 24.1 | 260 | 2.6 | 9819 | 100 |
| 1967 | 4715 | 50.0 | 1711 | 18.1 | 70 | 0.7 | 1458 | 15.5 | 230 | 2.4 | 9431 | 100 |
| 1970 | 7066 | 61.2 | 2163 | 18.7 | 35 | 0.3 | 503 | 4.4 | 212 | 1.8 | 11539 | 100 |

[a]West Germany only.

Sources: Statistical Abstracts of Sweden, 1960 (Stockholm: Nordstedts, 1961).
Befolkingsforandringar 1961-1970, (Stockholm: Nordstedts, 1973).

alone absorbs 70 percent of all foreigners residing in the Nordic region and 82 per cent of all Nordic migrants.

Table 2:9 shows that the number of foreigners receiving Swedish citizenship has remained fairly stable, around nine thousand a year, between 1955 and 1970. Thus, the last years have not seen any greater influx of new citizens than the earlier period. The growth pattern for former Nordic citizens is different, however, and has developed slowly throughout the period. In 1970, 61.2 percent of the new citizens were of Nordic origin, while in 1952 only 43.6 percent were. The EC countries, in contrast, have declined proportionally as a source of new citizens since 1961 and in 1970 accounted for only 18.7 percent. Great Britain and the U.S. are of marginal importance and only account for a few percentages. The Eastern European category is obviously affected by the recurrent influx of large numbers of refugees, who receive citizenship after several years of residence. Here the variations are considerable during the years, ranging from 38 percent in 1955 to 4.4 percent in 1970.

It seems that the most important and consistently large group of new Swedish citizens throughout the years is the Nordic group. This category has also become more relevant over time, as an ever larger share of the individuals are drawn from this region. So it seems that the inter-Nordic migration results in more permanent transfers of people across the national boundaries than do the extra-regional exchanges. This tendency also has become somewhat more noticeable during the last years, as a greater percentage of new citizens are of Nordic origin.

In order to supplement our basic migration data and to get a view of transactions among the societies at the elite level, we will study student exchanges. Again we will focus on Sweden, the country receiving the vast majority of all foreign students studying in the Nordic countries. It is of interest to ascertain if Nordic students study in Sweden in greater number than individuals from other regions. Foreign students often will hold key positions in their home countries after their period of study abroad. As such, they can sometimes act as important links between their homes and the place of study.

We see in Table 2:10 that the number of newly enrolled foreign students at Swedish universities has increased ten times between 1956 and 1971. Of particular interest is the sharp increase of students from

TABLE 2:10

NEWLY ENROLLED FOREIGN STUDENTS IN SWEDISH UNIVERSITIES 1956-1971

| Academic Year | Nordic N | % | EEC N | % | Great Britain N | % | East Europe N | % | USA N | % | Afro-Asia N | % | World N | % |
|---|---|---|---|---|---|---|---|---|---|---|---|---|---|---|
| 56/57 | 53 | 23.2 | 76 | 30.7 | 6 | 2.6 | 23 | 10.0 | 13 | 5.7 | 27 | 11.8 | 228 | 100 |
| 61/62 | 99 | 28.0 | 68 | 12.5 | 24 | 6.8 | 46 | 13.0 | 66 | 18.7 | 32 | 9.1 | 353 | 100 |
| 66/67 | 240 | 20.8 | 186 | 11.9 | 49 | 4.2 | 115 | 10.0 | 263 | 22.8 | 167 | 14.5 | 1154 | 100 |
| 71/72 | 839 | 35.6 | 193 | 5.4 | 65 | 2.8 | 297 | 12.6 | 314 | 13.3 | 290 | 12.3 | 2355[a] | 100 |

[a]This makes for 6.4 percent of all newly enrolled students in that year (36,604 total).

Sources: Hogre Studier, 1956/57-1961/62 (Stockholm: Nordstedts, 1959-1964). Unpublished statistics provided by the Swedish Central Bureau of Statistics, Stockholm.

other Nordic countries during this time period. In 1971-72 there were sixteen times as many newly enrolled Nordic students as in 1956-57. We also note the steep proportional decline of students from the EC countries, and the very marginal role of British students. Eastern Europe has provided a substantial number of students to the Swedish universities and maintains a ratio of 10 to 12 percent. Likewise, the U.S. and various Afro-Asian countries send increasing numbers of students to the universities. However, the largest proportion of foreign students are those holding other Nordic citizenships. This category has changed from 23 percent in 1956-57 to 36 percent in 1971-72. Thus, the Nordic exchanges dominate the transfers of people also at this elite level, and make for more intensive transactions within the region than between it and any external areas.

On the whole we find impressive transactions among the Nordic societies in comparison with external exchanges. Only Iceland is, in some areas, an exception to the general trend of clear Nordic dominance in the orientation of flows. This very small country, somewhat isolated from the rest of the region, has significant transactional ties with the U.S.A., Great Britain, and the continental European countries, which compete with the Nordic links. Similarly, Denmark has closer communication, migration, and trade links with the EC countries than does the rest of the region. In spite of these differences among societies, the general impression is of a region closely knit together in networks of transactions covering several types of transfers. No doubt the Nordic societies are extremely relevant to each other and in some areas, such as trade, are becoming even more so. The Nordic links clearly outweigh any external ties in the areas investigated here, and thus suggest the existence of a Nordic transnational community.

## Interest Groups

In addition to analyzing Nordic transaction flows we shall study the regional activities of various nongovernmental elites and organizations. According to recent studies by the Norwegian scholar Abraham Hallenstvedt, in 1971-72 there were 436 nongovernmental organizations with members from at least three of the countries in the region. In Table 2:11 we have categorized these organizations according to the type of activity they engage in. We see that about one third are concerned with business related

## DISTRIBUTION OF NORIDC AND GLOBAL NON-GOVERNMENTAL ORGANIZATIONS BETWEEN FUNCTIONAL CATEGORIES OF ACTIVITY

| Functional Area of Operation | Nordic | | Global | |
|---|---|---|---|---|
| Industry-Commerce | 154 | 35% | 562 | 29% |
| Industrial | 45 | | | |
| Agriculture, Fishery, Forestry | 37 | | | |
| Technical | 25 | | | |
| Trade | 24 | | | |
| Banking, Insurance, Transport | 23 | | | |
| | | | | |
| Workers-Employers | 137 | 31% | 182 | 9% |
| Labor, Professional Assoc. | 133 | | | |
| Employers | 4 | | | |
| | | | | |
| Other Social Areas | 145 | 33% | 1195 | 62% |
| Sport, Youth, Leisure | 49 | | | |
| Humanitarian, Social Service | 35 | | | |
| Scientific, Culture, International | 33 | | | |
| Party Groups | 17 | | | |
| Religious | 16 | | | |
| Total | 436 | 99% | 1939 | 100% |

Sources: Abraham Hallenstvedt, "Nordisk Foreningsliv: Omfang og Karakter," paper given at the Seminar on Nordic Organizations, Gothenbourg, Sweden, May 1974. Werner Feld, Nongovernmental Forces and World Politics (New York: Praeger, 1972), p. 181, Table 6:1.

activities, one third with relations between workers and employers, and another third with various other social concerns. The single most important category seems to be the Nordic labor unions and professional associations, which together make up 133 regional organizations.

When compared with global organizations, one notes that the Nordic organizations are oriented, to a greater extent, toward the economic sector of society such as business and labor. One could argue from this table that the Nordic NGOs are mainly interest-group oriented, while global organizations are in general primarily concerned with promoting more broadly defined causes and social concerns. We can then assert that the impact of the Nordic NGOs on their societies is more direct and penetrating than what is often the case for global NGOs.

The most active Nordic interest groups are the labor unions. Throughout this century the national organizations representing organized labor have met on a regional basis to exchange information and develop common strategies. The first such Nordic meeting took place as early as 1886. Since that time, continuous contacts have been maintained through formal congresses and intensive informal interactions. This tradition of close Nordic cooperation in the labor movement has had particular significance, as the unions have been closely affiliated with the Social Democratic parties in the region. These parties have dominated the political scene in the area since the 1930s and have had a considerable impact on the social and economic transformation in these countries.

For a long time, regional labor contacts were carried out through periodic short conferences and various irregular and informal exchanges among the labor leaders. The intensity of the interactions increased during the post-war period as the Nordic societies became more relevant to each other. For example, the establishment of a common labor market, the growth of multinational corporations, and a growing concern with influencing international developments affecting the Nordic region, made for increased regional contacts among the labor groups. Finally, in 1972 the national Federations of Labor in the five countries established the Council of Nordic Trade Unions to serve as a structured umbrella organization for the region.

This fairly new organization is headed by a Board of Directors, made up of two representatives from each of the participating eight national associations. This board meets several times per year to make decisions on a joint policy. The Council is serviced by a small secretariat, which is financed by contributions from the members and runs the daily affairs of the organization. The joint annual budget is about $150,000, which amounts to about three cents per individual member.

Due to the creation of a permanent joint secretariat, the continuity, intensity, and impact of the transnational interactions seems to have increased during recent years. Now, the regional effort is increasingly oriented toward finding joint policy solutions and making joint declarations on issues rather than merely exchanging information and ideas of mutual interest. A third phase of regional coordination of negotiations with employers is also slowly emerging in some areas.

According to the statutes of the Council of Nordic Trade Unions, the organization has several objectives. One purpose is to serve as a central clearing-house for the exchange of information on various topics of interest to the labor movement. Here the need is not only to keep up with regional developments but also with external events. For example, according to one source, the primary motive behind the Norwegian desire to form the Council was to get access to reliable information on conditions inside the EC.

A second goal is to reach agreements on joint policy in various areas of importance. During this process of bargaining in the Board of Directors' meetings, the secretariat serves in an important mediatory role to facilitate joint solutions. As the national leaderships usually are represented on the Board, decisions worked out there are accepted also in the national organizations. One important feature of this ambition to reach joint positions on policy is the decision to let the Council be the official forum for formulating responses to governmental requests for opinions (remiss) on various regional issues. Likewise, the Council has requested to participate in committee meetings of the Nordic Council and Council of Ministers as observers. The idea is that the tradition of interest group participation in government, which is dominant on the national scenes, should also operate on regional issues through the "co-opting" of the Council of Nordic Trade Unions into the joint public policy-making process.

The external dimension of joint policy solutions is also of importance to the organization. It is recognized that the Nordic labor unions by themselves are relatively small and without major input in the international or European labor federations. However, the joint Council represents five million workers and can have a considerable influence on decisions reached in these international forums. For this reason, the Nordic unions have joint representation through the Council in various international organizations. Generally, the Nordic representatives meet two hours before the international meeting begins and work out a joint position on the agenda issues. This way, the Nordic group can greatly increase the potential for having an impact on international developments. In particular, their united front in the European Labor Association is important as a counterweight to the unions of southern Europe.

A final purpose of the Council is to undertake studies on topical regional issues, such as multinational corporations, the working environment, family policy, and industrial democracy. Conferences on these subjects are held and committees work out policy statements on the basis of research sponsored by the organization. Through this process, continuous regional contacts are maintained throughout the policy-making sequences and joint solutions are then more easily found in the final stage of formal decision-making.

It seems obvious from this short account that the Nordic labor unions today are involved in a rather intensive network of interactions across national boudaries. The major difference from the past is that in the earlier period there were no more than two or three meetings each year, while today working meetings are held every month among representatives of the national groups. However, the reality is even more complex than has been discussed thus far. The Council of Nordic Trade Unions is the umbrella organization for just the national head organizations. Many of the separate national unions, representing particular sectors of the labor movement, have their own Nordic structures. These Nordic organizations are less formalized and often lack a central secretariat. Instead, they deal with more specific questions of direct relevance to the particular worker groups participating.

A 1973 listing included 36 such Nordic organizations of workers or employees which had joint secretariats in addition to the broad Council of Nordic Trade Unions. In fact, in some cases the activities at this level are as intense as and older than those of the head organizations themselves. For example, since 1968 the Nordic organizations of Metal Workers have had a joint secretariat with a budget of about $100,000 to promote regional interactions. The Board of Directors meet as often as every other month in formal meetings and its members are in nearly continuous contact by telephone. The objectives of information exchange, joint policy positions, and international representation, are dominant. Most of the other Nordic organizations listed have similar functions to perform, although they have fewer resources and their activities are less intensive than for this group representing 800,000 workers.

One indication that the regional labor interactions go beyond mere information exchanges and consultations is the fact that many organizations have mutual agreements to support unions in the other Nordic countries in times of strikes or lockouts. For example, during the Finnish Metal Workers conflict in 1971, which lasted for six weeks, the Nordic contributions accounted for half of the financial support paid by the Finnish union to its members. These Nordic payments are arranged through temporary loans by their counterparts in the other countries to ensure sufficient financial resources available to endure a prolonged conflict. This scheme enables many financially weak unions to fight more effectively for their objectives.

The Nordic labor movement is by no means the only interest group which is involved in regional transnational activities. However, its structural complexity and level of formal interactions are the greatest. The Nordic Employers' Federation is another group in which regional interactions have been taking place for a considerable period of time. As early as 1907 a Permanent Nordic Committee was established to serve as the major forum for regional deliberations. This committee is made up of the national presidents and directors general and meets once a year in formal session. In addition, the national staffs, including the directors general, meet periodically to coordinate major decisions regarding relations with the employees. Naturally, most of the regional interchanges take place informally, through mail or by telephone. In particular, this is the case for the staffs of the organizations. They have continuous contacts with their Nordic counterparts.

One gets the impression that the Nordic Employers, in contrast to the labor unions, try to avoid publicity and general awareness of their joint interactions and coordination. For example, it seems that the contacts among the national leaders are as intensive as for the labor leaders, but these are channeled primarily through informal means to avoid publicity. No joint secretariat or formal structure has been established by these groups, nor have any efforts been made to get joint representation in governmental bodies. However, in spite of these structural weaknesses, actual policy coordination and present-ation of joint positions also take place among these organizations. For example, there is a mutual obligation not to employ workers involved in labor conflicts with members in any of the other Nordic countries. "Confidential" annual reports are exchanged among the organizations each year to give detailed and valuable information on national developments to their counterparts. These reports contain aspects and statements not included in the annual reviews presented to the national memberships. It seems very interesting that the organ-izations feel close enough to give each other types of information that they withhold from their own members. On the international scene, the Nordic employers cooperate extensively and have a joint representative in the International Labour Organization in Geneva.

The major objective behind the regional activities seem to be to facilitate a united, stronger front against the extensive collaboration effort of labor unions. These groups have a considerable impact on the societies, both through their own activities and through their great influence on governmental policy. To meet this challenge, the Nordic activities of the employers are mainly taking place among the national head organizations and through discrete, but effective means. The separate branch organizations do not involve themselves as heavily in transnational efforts but rather rely on the central administration for such ventures. Due to the very informal, flexible mode of collaboration used it is very hard to determine if in fact trans-Nordic activities have increased during recent years. There have not been any major structural changes that can be pointed to and evaluated as was the case with the labor unions. Moreover, interviews with officials involved in the trans-Nordic interactions do not indicate any major informal changes during the last years. However, one must keep in mind the continued desire by these organizations to play down such regional collaboration.

There are numerous other groups in the Nordic region that are involved in the same type of transnational interactions as labor and employer groups. The various Federations of Industry and the Agriculture and Fishery Associations, for example, are also active in such activities. The general trends of informality, small joint secretariats, if any at all, intensive consultations, and periodic formal meetings also characterize these organizations. Due to the rather different agricultural structures, policies, and needs of the Nordic countries, the joint policy coordination by the farm groups is not very great. In contrast, the Federations of Industry are in continuous contact to draw on each other's experiences and try to reach mutual solutions to regional problems. In most cases, the last ten years have also seen some changes in the structure and process of these transnational activities. Increased mutual relevance of the Nordic societies and a new awareness of the need for joint external representation have made for more intensive interactions and substantially more important joint tasks. As the regional activities of these organizations do not seem to differ markedly from the previously discussed groups, we will not comment further on them here. We have already established the general pattern of transnational activity in the region which is used by most Nordic interest groups.

## Business

Separately, the Nordic countries provide rather small markets often too limited to sustain the kind of specialized industry characteristic of advanced industrial economies. Similarly, the production capacity of each unit is limited by the relatively small work force. To compensate for the small domestic markets many companies engage heavily in exports. Also, to make up for the limited production capacity at home many companies conclude joint production agreements with industry in other countries or establish foreign subsidiaries. For the purpose of this study, it is of interest to analyze to what extent such transnational business collaboration takes place within the Nordic region. If the Nordic area were to be characterized as a distinct transnational business community, one would expect corporations to choose the Nordic countries as the primary targets for foreign expansion and cooperation.

In Table 2:12 we have presented some data on the spread of company subsidiaries among various countries. We see that to a considerable extent Nordic companies have their subsidiaries located in other Nordic countries. Only the EC countries are more important targets for Nordic corporate expansion. We can also see that Denmark is particularly oriented toward the European continent, while Norwegian corporations have fewer subsidiaries in that area. If we turn the picture around and see what foreign countries dominate as the most prevalent home bases for subsidiaries operating in the Nordic region, we find that other Nordic countries are the most common for all countries except Sweden. The major external area is the U.S., which provides the home base for more corporations than the EC or Great Britain. On the whole, we find the Nordic societies to be tied together in an extensive network of parent companies and subsidiaries transcending national boundaries. Sweden alone accounts for two-thirds of the parent companies from Nordic countries and is very dominant in this respect in the region. However, the internal relations are not quite as extensive as for the EC region, and the area

TABLE 2:12

NUMBER OF PARENT COMPANIES FROM VARIOUS COUNTRIES HAVING SUBSIDIARIES AND ASSOCIATES IN GIVEN FOREIGN COUNTRIES 1970
(Percentages of distribution of companies among countries)

| Subsid/Parent | Denmark | Norway | Sweden | Nordic | EEC-Countries | Great Britain | USA | Total |
|---|---|---|---|---|---|---|---|---|
| A. Where Companies Have Subsidiaries | | | | | | | | |
| Denmark | – | 10.9 | 9.0 | 7.4 | 1.0 | 1.1 | 1.1 | 1.5 |
| Norway | 6.8 | – | 9.0 | 7.4 | 0.6 | 0.6 | 0.7 | 1.1 |
| Sweden | 13.0 | 20.0 | – | 5.2 | 1.5 | 1.5 | 1.8 | 1.9 |
| Finland | 2.3 | 1.4 | 6.4 | 4.9 | 0.2 | 0.3 | 0.4 | 0.6 |
| Nordic | 22.5 | 32.3 | 24.4 | 24.9 | 3.3 | 3.5 | 3.9 | 5.1 |
| EEC-Countries | 36.4 | 21.8 | 26.3 | 27.8 | 31.8 | 19.0 | 27.9 | 27.9 |
| Great Britain | 11.0 | 10.0 | 7.9 | 8.8 | 5.9 | – | 14.1 | 7.5 |
| USA | 3.6 | 5.5 | 5.7 | 5.3 | 4.4 | 6.8 | – | 3.5 |
| Total | 100.0 | 100.0 | 100.0 | 100.0 | 100.0 | 100.0 | 100.0 | 100.0 |
| B. Where Subsidiaries Have Parent Companies | | | | | | | | |
| Denmark | – | 6.0 | 25.9 | 31.9 | 18.2 | 20.0 | 24.9 | 100.0 |
| Norway | 8.1 | – | 35.3 | 43.4 | 14.6 | 15.6 | 21.4 | 100.0 |
| Sweden | 8.9 | 8.5 | – | 17.4 | 21.3 | 20.7 | 33.9 | 100.0 |
| Finland | 4.5 | 1.7 | 42.0 | 48.2 | 8.5 | 11.9 | 23.3 | 100.0 |
| Nordic | 5.6 | 5.1 | 20.3 | 31.9 | 17.4 | 18.3 | 27.3 | 100.0 |
| EEC-Countries | 1.7 | 0.6 | 4.0 | 6.3 | 29.9 | 17.8 | 35.6 | 100.0 |
| Great Britain | 1.9 | 1.1 | 4.4 | 7.4 | 20.8 | – | 66.5 | 100.0 |
| USA | 1.4 | 1.3 | 6.9 | 9.6 | 32.8 | 50.3 | – | 100.0 |
| Total | 1.3 | 0.8 | 4.2 | 6.3 | 26.3 | 26.1 | 35.5 | 100.0 |

Source: Yearbook of International Organization 1970-71 (Brussels: Union of International Organizations, 1971), p. 1031.

is somewhat more penetrated by external companies than the EC group
is.

The significance of the Nordic corporate ties is more noteworthy
if one considers the relatively limited size of the Nordic area when compared to external regions.  In addition, one must keep in mind the desire
of Nordic corporations to get inside the EC customs barrier as a force
behind establishing subsidiaries on the continent.  Such an objective is
not involved in Nordic corporate expansion, which instead is induced
by other reasons, such as a desire to take advantage of available production capacity in the neighboring countries.  Also, Swedish companies
have not been forced to compensate fully for their labor shortage by
creating production facilities abroad as they have been able to import
large quantities of workers from Finland.

In Table 2:13 we focus on the dominant country in the region,
Sweden.  We here see that in terms of the number of subsidiaries,
Nordic corporate ties account for over one-fourth of all transnational
links.  In contrast, when comparing the size of these ties in terms of
the number of employees involved, the Nordic connection is less
impressive.  Overall, the proportional share of Nordic companies is
high when one considers the limited size of most of these corporations
and economies.

An important feature of Nordic business collaboration is the
system of using partial contractors form the Nordic region in the
production of major articles.  For example, the automobile manu-
facturer, Volvo, is heavily dependent on contractors in Norway for
a major part of its production.  Many of the small companies
specializing in a single product to stay competive are tied up with
the industrial giants through such contracts.  It is estimated  that·
in Sweden this type of contracted production accounts for one
fourth of the total volume of mechanical output. [1]  Although the
national orientation of suppliers and producers in this system is
still dominant, the Nordic region as a whole is increasingly used
as a market and source of production.

To facilitate these trans-Nordic exchanges the Associations of
Mechanical Industry in the countries have established a joint "Nordic
contractor exchange".  This exchange has been operating since 1966
and has greatly enhanced the possibilities for finding suitable contractors

TABLE 2:13

## SWEDISH CORPORATIONS ABROAD AND FOREIGN CORPORATIONS IN SWEDEN 1974

| Country of Operation of Swedish Corporations | Number of Subsidiaries | | Number of Employees | |
|---|---|---|---|---|
| Denmark | 260 | 11% | 13.950 | 4% |
| Finland | 176 | 7% | 13.513 | 4% |
| Norway | 237 | 10% | 11.826 | 4% |
| Total Nordic | 673 | 27% | 39.289 | 12% |
| EEC-countries | 975 | 40% | 144.051 | 45% |
| USA | 151 | 6% | 16.781 | 5% |
| Other Areas | 657 | 27% | 118.020 | 37% |
| Total | 2456 | 100% | 318.141 | 100% |

| Home Country of Foreign Corporations in Sweden | Number of Corporations | | Number of Employees | |
|---|---|---|---|---|
| Denmark | 142 | 12% | 7.746 | 8% |
| Finland | 69 | 6% | 2.070 | 2% |
| Norway | 96 | 8% | 3.922 | 4% |
| Total Nordic | 307 | 26% | 13.738 | 14% |
| EEC-countries | 431 | 36% | 38.597 | 38% |
| USA | 309 | 26% | 40.386 | 40% |
| Other Areas | 156 | 13% | 8.129 | 8% |
| Total | 1203 | 100% | 100.850 | 100% |

Source: Svante Iger, Den svenska ekonomins internationalisering, Rapport No. 206, Sekretariatet for Framtisdsstudier, Stockholm, 1976, pp. 48,61.

or customers in need of suppliers. A newsletter listing available space and current needs is distributed periodically to the 4500 member corporations of the associations. In the period 1966-1973, 4593 notices of free capacity and 2419 requests for suppliers were transmitted through this newsletter to Nordic corporations.[2] Of these, Sweden alone accounted for 72 percent of the requests for contractors and 39 percent of the notices of free space. Most likely, additional contacts were made by corporations which previously had benefitted from the exchange and established relations on their own. We do not know how many of these advertised notices and requests actually resulted in successful contracts, but judging from the popularity of the scheme, it appears to have been generally beneficial. A survey of 235 Swedish companies in 1968, two years after the creation of the Nordic exchange, shows that 105 corporations had used the exchange and that 70 of the 105 had established new business contacts through it.[3] Obviously, this means of establishing contacts throughout the Nordic region has been used fairly extensively by industry and most likely resulted in many new transnational relations among Nordic corporations.

In addition to the tradition of production sharing, Nordic corporations collaborate by many other means to compensate for their relatively small size compared to European or American enterprises. Cooperation takes place in various areas, such as technical development, financing, export, and joint purchases in the world market. Several companies have pooled their resources in joint trans-Nordic projects to develop new products and manufacturing techniques. The new Nordic Fund for Industrial Development has specifically been created to encourage and help finance such joint undertakings by industry. Several Nordic banks have established joint affiliates abroad to help finance Nordic industry and export. The sizeable Norwegian shipping fleet has largely been built in Sweden, where long-term financing has also been available. Some export oriented industries,such as textile and mechanical producers, have united in efforts to reach the international market. Joint export organizations have then been established for all companies which market their products under a single brand name. Similarly, some Nordic corporations, such as the Nordic Cooperative Associations, act as one buyer in the world market to get a better price and higher quality.

\*\*\*\*\*\*\*\*\*\*\*\*\*\*\*\*

In this chapter we have seen how the North European region in many respects constitutes a distinct transnational community. A trade community was indicated by intense exchanges of goods in the region, while the flow of messages pointed to a communications community. Similarly, the movement of people across national borders was more intensive and long-term within the region than between this and other areas. Several national interest groups were found to engage in transnational activities on a regional scale and Nordic business collaboration was used to expand beyond the small national economies.

In all ᴜne areas discussed, the activities reached beyond the jurisdiction of any one political unit. Apparently, the political configuration of the region seems to be constantly undermined by nongovernmental forces and actors. No doubt the Nordic governments have realized the potential threat to their effective authority over, and control of, societal change and stability caused by this development. In the next chapter we shall discuss how the North European governments have responded to the challenge posed by transnationalism and see what techniques they have adopted to manage these forces.

# 3. The Collective Management Process

Rolf Edberg, a prominent promoter of Nordic cooperation, once compared national boundaries to hinges. Rather than perceiving borders as obstacles separating national units one should view them as hinges which connect distinct entities. To Edberg, the governments of these political units have a special responsibility to ensure that these hinges are well greased to facilitate mutually rewarding transnational exchanges.[1] This attitude toward transnational collaboration is very common in Northern Europe and helps explain why the Nordic political elites have successfully engaged in intimate collective management of transnationalism and have yet maintained their distinct national identies.

In recent years, an additional concern has given a further incentive to collaboration. It has been realized that domestic economic and social conditions in Northern Europe are highly sensitive to changes in the international environment. As all Nordic governments take an activist attitude toward societal management, it has been frustrating for the political leaderships to be inhibited in their domestic policy tasks by restraining external developments. The feeling that one can not successfully manage or control domestic change without also having some impact on international developments has become prevalent. To achieve this objective of better controlling their environment, the North European governments have seen the advantages of collective effort.

North European developments can be managed by direct cooperation among the governments aimed at reducing potentially disturbing impact from the immediate external environment. Broader European and global forces can also be faced better collectively. Through joint representation in international forums and through joint policy stands on many issues, the Nordic governments have

43

increased their leverage in international negotiations. This has improved the chances for the creation of a more favorable international climate. So, by joint international representation combined with regional coordination, the national political elites hope to improve their capacity to control their own societies.

In the following pages we shall outline the means used by the North European political elites to manage their immediate regional environment. In the previous chapter, we showed how the North European region constitutes a distinct transnational community characterized by extensive transactions as well as intensive group interactions across national boundaries. These transnational forces have the potential to seriously hamper unilateral national political steering. The objective of the collective management effort is to facilitate the transnational flows, i.e. grease the hinges, as each society has come to depend on them for continued affluence and prosperity. But is is also crucial to ensure that these flows will not weaken the governments' ability to plan for the future of their societies. In other words, the political elites encourage transnationalism but they want to be in full control of these activities so their authority will not be undermined.

## Structural Framework for Collective Management

Since its first session in Copenhagen in 1953, the Nordic Council has served as the major institution of Nordic cooperation. In fact, to many outside observers it has been the only joint structure worth studying in the region. This is an unfortunate attitude, however, because throughout the post-war ear, numerous less prominent, yet important joint institutions have existed alongside the Nordic Council.

While the Nordic Council serves as the major forum for parliamentary discussion and resolutions to the respective governments, many of the less well-known organs function at the ministerial level to cordinate their activities. For example, numerous committees and commissions like the Nordic Cultural Commission, the Nordic Economic Cooperation Committee, the Nordic Uniform Law Committee, the Nordic Social Welfare Committee, etc., have functioned at the ministerial level quite independently of the Nordic Council. In fact, many of these smaller, more specialized structures were

FIGURE 3:1

NORDIC INSTITUTIONAL STRUCTURE 1977

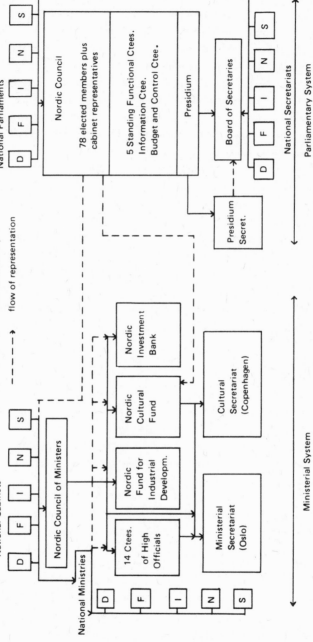

established before the Nordic Council was instituted. Since 1971 many of these bodies have gradually been incorporated as separate committees under the then established Nordic Council of Ministers.

In 1977, there were fourteen such permanent committees of national civil servants operating under the auspices of thé Council of Ministers. This can be compared with eight committees and working groups in the parliamentary sphere under the Nordic Council. It is obvious even from these simple figures that one cannot identify the Nordic regional institutional structure solely in terms of the Nordic Council itself. However, the actual situation is even more complex than this, as it is only a small proportion of the total number of joint organs that are incorporated in the Nordic Council or Council of Ministers systems. It is fair to say that no one knows exactly how many joint institutions exist in the region today, but the most recent and reliable listing includes no less than 83 permanent governmental organs of Nordic cooperation in addition to the 22 committees already mentioned.[2] We are thus faced with a complex set of small, decentralized institutions, each functioning within its particular field of operation, and making the Nordic institutional structure rather hard to analyze in its entirety.

In order to get a broad view of the contemporary situation, it might be useful to outline the structure of the Nordic Council and the Council of Ministers. These two institutions, having several smaller units within them, constitute the major parts of the Nordic institutional structure today. This is true with respect to size, budget allocations, staffs' scope of activities covered, involvement of national political leaders, and public awareness of the organs. Although we cannot disregard the numerous smaller organs mentioned above, we can temporarily ignore them to draw a somewhat simplified picture of the Nordic structures.

The five national parliaments are represented in the Nordic Council. This body of 78 elected members, plus additional representatives of the cabinets, serves as the major Nordic legislative organ. It is of interest that since its establishment in 1952, the Nordic Council has included cabinet representatives as non-voting members in its proceedings to ensure a close and efficient working relationship between legislative proposals and ministerial decisions and implementation. Five Standing Committees carry the major legislative burdens of evaluating

46

and commenting on proposals and reports. In addition, two special working groups have been established for information activities and for parliamentary control of ministerial budgets.

The Presidium of the Council, consisting of one representative for each parliament, superivses and directs the Council. In a sense, this body can be seen as a governing board for the Council with several important powers delegated to it. Each national delegation is assisted by a Secretary with a small staff. In addition to the five national Secretariats, the Presidium is served by its own Secretariat consisting of truly joint Nordic officials. This Presidium Secretariat handles the various common tasks of the Council, such as budgets, publications, contacts with the Council of Ministers, information, and preparation for the many meetings. The Presidium Secretary together with the five national Secretaries General form a Board of Secretaries, which is in almost constant contact, to plan, prepare, and carry out the many day-to-day decisions of the Council. This group of civil servants has considerable powers delegated to it by the Presidium to supervise and implement most routine tasks of the Council. In addition, their advice and recommendations carry considerable weight in formal decisions by the Presidium on many important matters.

Finally, each of the five Standing Committees has one secretary to aid the committee in its work. These committee secretaries are under the direction of the Presidium Secretary and are appointed by the Presidium. Thus, the main structural features of the Nordic legislative institution i.e. the Nordic Council, are: five Standing Committees and two Working Groups for the legislative work, the Presidium to supervise, and several secretaries to implement and direct everyday activities.

The major efforts toward Nordic cooperation at the ministerial level have been handled outside the Nordic Council system. In 1971, a formal structure to coordinate and implement inter-Nordic activities by the national cabinets was established in the Nordic Council of Ministers. Since 1971, national ministers have been meeting regularly in this Council to make efforts toward Nordic cooperation. The composition of the Council varies according to the functional area of the questions discussed. In addition, each cabinet has appointed one Minister to be responsible for Nordic cooperation in general.

These Ministers of Cooperation meet quite often to coordinate, supervise and plan the various efforts toward Nordic cooperation in the specific functional areas, as handled by the other Ministers.

The Council of Ministers is assisted by several Permanent Committees of High Officials who prepare the meetings, decisions, and proposals of the Council. These Permanent Committees are made up of high ranking civil servants in the various national Ministries and meet frequently to keep the Nordic activities flowing. Also, one of these, the Committee of Deputies, is charged with general supervision, coordination, and planning functions and meets as often as once a month.

The various Ministers and High officials are assisted by two Nordic Secretariats handling the day-to-day activities of Nordic Ministerial cooperation. A Cultural Secretariat in Copenhagen handles the broadly defined cultural activities of Nordic cooperation, while the Secretariat of the Council of Ministers in Oslo deals with all remaining aspects. This division of the Secretarial duties into two separate organs is a result of the piecemeal establishment of the Council of Ministers system throughout several years.

Two grant giving funds to promote Nordic cooperation projects exist at this level. The Nordic Cultural Fund, established in 1966, promotes cultural schemes, while the Nordic Fund for Industrial Development, established in 1973, assists technical projects for regional industrial innovations. While the Cultural Fund is served by the Cultural Secretariat in Copenhagen, the Industrial Development Fund has its own small secretariat in Stockholm. Decisions on awards are made by representatives from the national governments on the basis of majority vote. The Cultural Fund has an annual grant giving capacity of approximately 1.5 million dollars and the Industrial Fund about 2.5 million dollars.

In 1975, a Nordic Investment Bank was created, which began operations the following year. With a basic capital of 400 million Special Drawing Rights (SDR) and a total lending capacity of 1000 million SDRs, the bank helps finance investments of interest to at least two Nordic countries. The bank is located in Helsinki and is governed by a Board of Directors made up of two representatives for each of the five participating governments. Decisions on loans are made by qualified majority vote (7 out of 10 is required), where each representative is given one vote. Subsequently, Sweden which contributed 40% of the capital to the bank has the same voting strength as Iceland which contributes only 1%.

## Participants In Collective Management

Our next task is to identify the regional actors involved in the collective management effect. National and Nordic officials, politicians, ministers and parliamentarians are all participants in this process of joint policy-making. The national cabinets are represented by the various ministers. It is assumed here that the national minister speaks for his entire cabinet in his dealings with other ministers.[3] Thus, political decisions are taken at this ministerial level in a traditional inter-governmental manner.

Below each national minister numerous officials participate in the joint management process. These civil servants are supposed to serve their ministers and speak for them in their dealings with their regional counterparts. Naturally, the degree of political control over the activities of the national officials varies among ministries and countries. In most cases, the ministers are heavily dependent on their staff for advice, information, and suggestions for decisions. This is particularly the case in Nordic affairs, as the top leadership in each national agency can only devote a very minor part of its attention to Nordic cooperation problems. The factual situation then is that the national officials have considerable independence vis-a-vis their political employers and should be regarded as separate types of actors.

There is a third group of national actors to be considered, namely the national parliamentarians meeting in the Nordic Council. These actors have no obligation to act on behalf of their government, as they are not part of the cabinet and are often in opposition. In practice, the parliamentarians have great freedom of choice in their decisions. Judging from interviews with these parliamentarians, neither their national constituencies nor their parties generally make any demands on them to act in a certain manner in their Nordic activities.

The national Secretaries General of the Nordic Council, serving the national delegations, will be treated together with the joint officials

49

of the Presidium Secretariat as Nordic parliamentary officials. The formal difference in employment between these two types of parliamentary servants does not correspond to any greater practical difference in their roles or outlooks as actors in the regional process. Generally, the national Secretaries General have placed as much emphasis on penetrating their national bureaucracies with Nordic sentiments, ideas, and solutions as to represent strictly national interests in the Council. In taking this approach, they have not differed much from the major concern of the officials of the Presidium Secretariat. Although these two sets of parliamentary officials are under the formal direction of the parliamentary delegates to the Nordic Council, we have already pointed to their great freedom of maneuver and independence of their employers. Thus, they constitute one important type of actor in the regional cooperation process.

On the ministerial side, since 1972 there have also been Nordic officials formally independent of any of the national governments. These officials correspond most closely to the international civil servants whom we are familiar with in various global and regional governmental organizations. We then have five different types of actors to consider in the Nordic region. They are: the national ministers, the national officials, the national parliamentarians, the Nordic parliamentary officials, and the Nordic ministerial officials. In the following analysis, we will show how each type interacts and what roles the various actors play in the joint policy-making process.

## Forms and Means of Interaction

The regional actors interact formally in various joint meetings throughout the year. The national and Nordic actors in the parliamentary sphere meet regularly in the five Standing Committees of the Nordic Council, the Presidium, the annual session, and in several other select forums. During 1974 there were about 35 meetings held in this sphere as compared to approximately 20 in 1964.[4]

The Nordic cabinets interact in various meetings of ministers. This form of interaction was established long before the creation of the Nordic Council of Ministers in 1971. As early as the inter-war period, some Nordic ministers met regularly to exchange views and

TABLE 3:1

NORDIC MEETINGS 1962-1973

| Time Period | Parliamentarian Meetings | | Ministerial Meetings | | National Officials Meetings | | Total Meetings | |
|---|---|---|---|---|---|---|---|---|
| | N | % | N | % | N | % | N | % |
| 1962-1964 | 59 | 17.3 | 40 | 24.2 | 248 | 24.8 | 347 | 23.0 |
| 1965-1967 | 75 | 22.0 | 29 | 17.6 | 151 | 15.1 | 255 | 16.9 |
| 1968-1970 | 81 | 23.8 | 41 | 24.8 | 314 | 31.3 | 436 | 28.9 |
| 1971-1973 | 126 | 37.0 | 55 | 33.3 | 289 | 28.8 | 470 | 31.2 |
| 1962-1973 | 341 | 100.0 | 165 | 100.0 | 1002 | 100.0 | 1508 | 100.0 |

Source: Nordic Council, Nordiskt Kalendarium, 1962-1974.

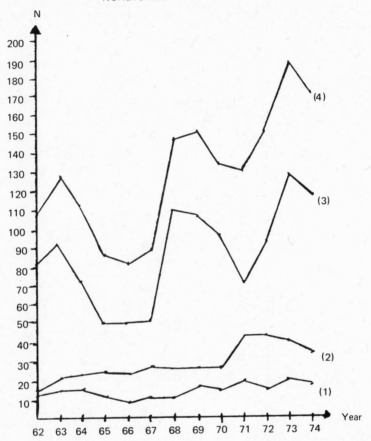

NORDIC MEETINGS 1962-1974

(1) Ministerial meetings; (2) Parliamentary meetings; (3) National officials' meetings; (4) Total meetings.

Source: Nordic Council, <u>Nordiskt Kalendarium</u> 1962-1974.

solve common problems. After World War II the scope and frequency of these meetings increased. Since 1971, many of these meetings have been held within the framework of the Council of Ministers, while others continue as separate ministerial meetings outside this more formal setting.

The most intensive interactions take place among the national civil servant who handle the day-to-day activities of Nordic cooperation in their ministry or governmental agency. In fact, there is not one week of the year that some group of national officials does not get together formally to discuss policy planning and decide on joint strategies. During recent years, these meetings have also included officials from the two Nordic secretariats serving the ministerial cooperation process.

We find Table 3:1 and Fig. 3:2 that the frequency of Nordic meetings has increased considerably during the last twelve years. While the number of ministerial meetings per year has remained fairly stable during the period, the parliamentarians have met more often since 1970. Obviously the reorganization and strengthening of the Nordic Council structure in 1971 has also been coupled with an increase in the interactions in this sphere. The frequency of Nordic meetings among national officials varies considerably between years. In 1962-63 the frequency was fairly high, during the next four years fewer meetings were held, while in the period 1968-70 intensive interaction took place. This two-year period of activity was then followed by a sudden drop in 1971 and then a gradual increase.

The stagnation of interactions during 1964-1967 can be attributed to the routine, low-key character of Nordic cooperation during these years, coupled with domestic concern over the relations with the EEC and EFTA. In 1968-70 the more frequent interactions took place at the time of the intensive NORDEK negotiations. The failure of completing the NORDEK treaty in the spring of 1970 resulted in a decline in Nordic interactions. Again, official attention was directed toward the Continent. However, following the political decision to strengthen the structures of Nordic governmental cooper-ation, the frequency of meetings among the national officials increased again as the new institutions began to operate. Apparently the great fluctuations in the frequency of meetings among national officials can be explained in terms of the political interests and activities during this twelve-year period. It seems that bureaucratic interaction and trans-governmental contacts are closely related to the political climate, interest, and leadership of the day and do not function separately from this political dimension.

If we make a comparison with the frequency of governmental meetings in the EEC, we find that this regional group has a far higher level of formal interactions. In 1970, 44½ days were spent in session of the Council of Ministers (other than agriculture), 153 days were spent in meetings of the Permanent Representatives Committee, and 1632½ days of meetings of various expert and other committees.[5] In addition, there were some 300 committee meetings of the European Parliament on top of about 45 days of plenary sessions.[6] These figures can be compared with the data in Table 3:1. We found that in the Nordic region there was an average of 125 meetings per year during 1962-1973. Of these, 28 were parliamentary meetings, 83 were meetings of national officials, and 14 were ministerial meetings (in general, a Nordic meeting lasts one full day). Obviously the number of meetings per year in the Nordic region is not very impressive when compared with the almost constant formal interaction in Brussels.[7]

How often on the average do the regional actors attend Nordic meetings? This question was included in a mail questionnaire sent to the leading national and Nordic actors involved in Nordic cooperation.[8] We see from Table 3:2 that 35% of the national actors, parliamentarians, and officials attend Nordic meetings at least once a month, and 12% at least twice a month. We also see that parliamentarians meet less often than officials. 40% of the national governmental officials meet with their Nordic counterparts at least once a month, while 27% of the parliamentarians do the same.

The number of Nordic meetings attended by Nordic officials is naturally higher since they generally participate in all meetings within their functional sphere. Table 3:3 shows that half of the Nordic officials attend five or more meetings per month. This is an average of at least one meeting per week. Also here, the highest frequency occurs in the ministerial sphere. While half of the Nordic parliamentary officials attend 2-4 meetings, two-thirds of the Nordic ministerial officials participate in five or more meetings each month.

The Nordic meetings have also tended to increase in frequency during the last years, particularly for the parliamentarians. The Nordic officials are naturally the most active in these interactions as they devote

## TABLE 3:2

## NUMBER OF NORDIC MEETINGS ATTENDED BY NATIONAL ACTORS

| Actor | Number of Meetings Attended During Last Six Months | | | | | | | | | | | | |
|---|---|---|---|---|---|---|---|---|---|---|---|---|
| | 0 | | 1-2 | | 3-5 | | 6-11 | | 12- | | Total | |
| | N | % | N | % | N | % | N | % | N | % | N | % |
| National Officials | 4 | 8 | 14 | 27 | 13 | 25 | 13 | 25 | 8 | 15 | 52 | 100 |
| Parliamentarians | 1 | 3 | 2 | 5 | 24 | 65 | 7 | 19 | 3 | 8 | 37 | 100 |
| National Actors | 5 | 6 | 16 | 18 | 37 | 42 | 20 | 23 | 11 | 12 | 89 | 100 |

Question: How many Nordic meetings did you attend during the last six months?

Source: Mail Questionnaire to National Actors, fall 1974.

TABLE 3:3

## NUMBER OF NORDIC MEETINGS ATTENDED BY NORDIC ACTORS

Question: How many Nordic meetings did you attend during the last month?

| Actor | Number of Meetings Attended During the Last Month | | | | | | | | | |
|---|---|---|---|---|---|---|---|---|---|---|
| | 0-1 | | 2-4 | | 5-9 | | 10- | | Total | |
| | N | % | N | % | N | % | N | % | N | % |
| Parliamentary Officials | 3 | 18 | 9 | 53 | 3 | 18 | 2 | 12 | 17 | 100 |
| Ministerial Officials | 1 | 5 | 5 | 26 | 10 | 53 | 3 | 16 | 19 | 100 |
| Nordic Actors | 4 | 11 | 14 | 39 | 13 | 36 | 5 | 14 | 36 | 100 |

Source: Mail Questionnaire to Nordic Officials, fall 1974.

their entire work load to Nordic cooperation. But it is also significant that the national officials in the national ministries and agencies meet frequently with their counterparts to discuss and decide on various cooperative ventures.

Written correspondence is another important means of interaction and communication among the regional actors. Here the tradition of direct contact between the national agencies or ministries, without using the Foreign Ministry channels, has been most valuable to establish close working relations. In contrast to most other forms of external correspondence, the inter-Nordic exchanges take place directly between the interested parties themselves.[9] The rationale behind this practice is that Nordic issues are similar to and should be handled like domestic policy, and not become separated and external to this. As a result, even local authorities such as criminal courts, policy districts, municipal governments, etc., can and do communicate directly with their counterparts in neighboring countries.[10] After several recommendations by the Nordic Council during the 1950s to codify this practice, the Nordic governments finally legitimized the tradition of direct communication among governmental agencies in the 1962 Helsinki Agreement.

Naturally this practice has diminished the role of the Foreign Offices in Nordic affairs. It is also natural that the latter generally have been critical of direct communication. Their agrument has been that the Nordic countries are also 'foreign powers' where coordination and external consistency in policy are important to the national interest. As the situation now stands, the Foreign Ministries have only very limited opportunity to coordinate the Nordic policies and cannot hope to follow the numerous diverse activities in the area. Since the 1971 reorganization of the Nordic trans-governmental structure, their possibilities have been somewhat enhanced as they play a role in the new Council of Ministers system. Generally, the Foreign Ministries provide the staffs to the national coordination offices assisting the representatives in the Committee of Deputies. Yet, the practice of direct communications is well established in all Nordic governments, and the Foreign Ministry is only one among many agencies involved in Nordic Affairs.

There is no way of knowing exactly how many letters are sent between the regional actors regarding Nordic cooperation issues. According to testimony by participants, the flow is heavy and con-

57

tinuous, reaching down into national administrations as well as across various functional agencies. It is highly probable that the growth in the exchange of written communications has stagnated during the last ten years, as the telephone is now frequently used. Possibly the use of written communications for decision-making and consultations among the national agencies saw its greatest utility during the 1950s and early 1960s.

A substantial number of regional exchanges, consultations, discussions, and decisions today take place on the telephone. During the 1960s the developing tele-technology made it possible to dial directly to all Nordic countries except Iceland. And so a national official can now quite easily pick up his phone and come into immediate contact with his counterpart in any of the other three Nordic countries. In many cases the members of the numerous Nordic committees can consult by telephone and make decisions on various issues without having to meet at any one place. This way quick decisions can be made in an informal and effective manner.

Due to the language similarities, close personal relations, speed, and low costs involved, the telephone is used far more frequently in inter-Nordic discussions than in contacts with other countries. A rough estimate is that about 70% of all international calls going through the central switchboard serving the Swedish ministries are to and from other Nordic countries.[11] In addition, about 200 of the highest officials in the Swedish ministries have private lines, not served by the switchboard, from which they can dial directly to the other Nordic countries except Iceland. As a result, the predominance of Nordic communications is even greater than the estimate of calls going through the central switchboard would indicate.

Table 3:4 shows some responses to our questionnaire and throws light on the frequency of inter-Nordic telephone interactions. We find that two-thirds of national officials call another Nordic country on the average at least once a week, and one-third at least twice a week. The parliamentarians do not interact as frequently as the national officials. One-third never called any other Nordic country during the last month, while half of them made from one to five calls during the month. It is obvious from these figures that national officials and, to a lesser extent, the parliamentarians, are in very frequent contact across national borders to handle Nordic policy problems jointly.

## TABLE 3:4

### NUMBER OF TRANS-NORDIC TELEPHONE CALLS BY NATIONAL ACTORS

Question: How many times did you call another Nordic country at work during the last month?

| Actor | Number of Calls Made During the Last Month | | | | | | | | | | | | | |
| --- | --- | --- | --- | --- | --- | --- | --- | --- | --- | --- | --- | --- | --- | --- |
| | 0 | | 1-2 | | 3-5 | | 6-10 | | 11-17 | | 18-22 | | Total | |
| | N | % | N | % | N | % | N | % | N | % | N | % | N | % |
| National Officials | 8 | 15 | 10 | 19 | 17 | 33 | 12 | 23 | 3 | 6 | 2 | 4 | 52 | 100 |
| Parliamentarians | 13 | 38 | 9 | 26 | 9 | 26 | 3 | 9 | 0 | 0 | 0 | 0 | 34 | 100 |
| National Actors | 21 | 24 | 19 | 22 | 26 | 30 | 15 | 17 | 3 | 3 | 2 | 2 | 86 | 100 |

Source: Mail Questionnaire to National Actors, fall 1974.

The fairly intensive network of telephone contacts can in part explain the relatively low frequency of formal meetings in the region. Often a meeting is not required to settle an issue, as deliberations can be made by telephone with each official still in his office. The savings in time, money, and manpower of this technique are obvious. The role of the Nordic officials is important here. They serve as a central clearing-house for regional contacts and make sure all parties are included, issues are kept alive, and decisions are reached. Although we do not have any statistical material on the frequency of telephone calling by these officials, we know from conversations with them and from personal observations that their telephones are constantly in use for interactions with national actors and other Nordic officials.

Finally, it should be emphasized that one major reason this informal means of interaction is used so extensively and works so smoothly is because of the tradition of regular meetings of the regional actors. They know each other well, both from the frequent formal discussions and from the commonly related social activities such as lunches, dinners, etc. The experiences of several years of professional and social relations naturally enhance feelings of familiarity, closeness, and often respect for the actors from the various countries. One major occasion when all the regional actors concerned with Nordic cooperation come together is the annual session of the Nordic Council. The "socialization" process during this week of meetings, dinners, receptions, and night-time activities is just as valuable for the numerous national and Nordic officials attending as for the parliamentary and ministerial delegates themselves. As a consequence of these personal relations, sufficient familiarity has developed to enable the joint decision-making process to work very smoothly is spite of its decentralized character.

We have discussed the forms and means of Nordic interaction among the regional actors, and have noted an increase in the frequency of formal meetings during the last twelve years. However, when compared with the Continental experience, the Nordic rates are unimpressive. Instead, the most important means of interaction during recent years has been the informal channels of communication. In particular, the use of the telephone should be stressed as a means both for consultation and decision. One interesting observation is that these networks of regional interactions exist across the national administrations rather than being channeled through any central, coordinating body. A pattern of transgovernmental relations seems to be present in the Nordic region.

## Norms Guiding the Collective Management Effort

We discussed in the preceding section the forms of regional interaction among the various actors involved in the collective management process. We were then struck by the importance of informal interactions in the region and the rather low ratio of formal meetings to actual policy results. One reason for this situation can undoubtedly be found in the norms guiding these regional interactions.

Many observers of Nordic politics have noted the prevalent norms of compromise, consensus, factual presentations, and discussion in the countries, which seem to facilitate the stable, harmonious, and gradual social and political development of the societies. Tom Anton, for example, describes the Swedish elite culture as one

> in which a highly pragmatic intellectual style, oriented toward the discovery of workable solutions to specific problems, structures a consensual approach to policy making . . . . Viewing politics as work, and following practices that encourage widespread consultation in decision-making, it is natural for the Swedish elite to think of politics in terms of cooperation rather than conflict.[12]

It seems reasonable that these norms, operating in the internal political process, would also be instrumental in the joint policy processes. This is particularly the case, as Nordic affairs in many respects are not seen or handled as international relations in general, but more like an extension of domestic policy making. Thus, inter-Nordic political bargaining and interactions generally resemble the continuous discussions and deliberations taking place among various national groups and organizations in national policy making.

This process can be characterized as being deliberative, rationalistic, open, and consensual. It includes long periods of deliberation on each issue by well-trained specialists, comprehensive rational review of possible alternatives, and an effort to get full information before decision-making. All parties with legitimate interest in the outcome are consulted. Final decisions are consensual, in the sense that they are seldom taken without the agreement of virtually all parties involved. The result of these features is a policy-making process that often is very slow, incremental, and without the excitement of distinct crisis or big decisions.[13]

Some analysts have pointed to the painstakingly slow cooperation process in the Nordic region, as compared with the quicker, more dramatic, political decisions made on the European Continent.[14] For example, deliberations and discussions about a Nordic Common Market took place throughout the 1950s. The only major result of these extensive efforts was a number of detailed studies of the possible effects of such an economic arrangement on the national societies.

When, in 1959, the governments were finally prepared to make a fianl decision on the issue, the situation in Europe had drastically changed and the Nordic option was largely overtaken by the larger European solutions.[15] Similarly, in 1968-1970, intensive deliberations over the creation of an economic union (NORDEK), resulted in final failure as once again broader European developments proceeded too fast for the Nordic policy-making process. Also on many smaller issues, Nordic investigatory committees are at work for several years before a final report is presented. For example, the period between original proposal in the Nordic Council and final governmental decision is often very long.

It is tempting to suggest from these examples, that the Nordic cooperation process is basically indecisive, slow, and primarily unsuccessful due to the lack of a sincere commitment to joint solutions by the governments in the region. However, the major reason behind these features of Nordic cooperation seems to be found in the policy-making cultures of the various countries. As can be expected, the intra-regional process is largely a reflection of the basic norms and values shaping the national policy-making processes. For example, only rarely have political decisions preceded intensive investigations and deliberations of each separate cooperation issue. This policy-making style should not be used as an indication of a low degree of national commitment to the joint ventures by the Nordic governments.

On most Nordic questions the political leaders of the countries are not directly involved in the decision-making process, but the various national and Nordic officials largely determine the outcomes. Therefore, it is of particular interest to analyze the norms guiding the activities at this bureaucratic level. The first point to be made is that the Nordic interactions more closely approximate intra-governmental discussions and bargaining than they do international negotiations. Although the national representatives usually are seated together in the formal meetings, no formal distinctions or signs of recognition are used to identify various governments. Instead, a fairly close-knit, relaxed, and informal group of governmental officials gets together in the Permanent Committees of High Officials for regular consultations. Although the representatives obviously come well prepared with definite views on most items of the agenda, they engage in fairly free and open discussion in the meetings.

The informal, relaxed, and intimate atmosphere is particularly noticeable in the parliamentary sphere, where the participants in no sense can be regarded as representing their particular governments. Here the similarity with a national political meeting seems the greatest. No doubt the language similarities are an important factor in inducing this informal, friendly, and close atmosphere among the national representatives. Most of the participants can be understood in their native language without the use of interpreters. An exception are the Icelandic and some of the Finnish members, who often are faced with difficulties not felt by the other delegates. The language situation also facilitates various forms of informal and social relations among different nationals.

The formal rule for decision among the Nordic governments is unanimity on substantive issues. In contrast, decisions in the Nordic Council are taken by majority vote. In practice, the prevailing decision norm is compromise and consensus formation in both spheres of operation. However, these terms can mean different things in different settings and must be further specified. For example, Ernst Haas has presented a scale, indicating different decision norms that are all subsumed under compromise. [16]

Formally, the norms used in the Nordic trans-governmental decision-making process would resemble Haas' lowest type: decision according to the lowest common denominator. The least cooperative actor would then determine the outcome of the decision. Although this impression seems true at first sight, we should look further into the consensual decision-making process. Two types of norms can be found here, both of which can be subsumed under consensus formation.

Decisions can be taken by active approval of all the parties involved or by the lack of active dissent by any of the parties concerned.

It seems fairly difficult to reach a decision when the active support of all the parties is required. This norm is prevalent in common decisions reached in an isolated bargaining setting by actors not also involved in other decision-making processes. In contrast, decisions based on the lack of active dissent are easier to come by as the parties do not have to support the decision as long as they do not strongly disapprove of it. This decision norm is prevalent among actors involved in continuous bargaining processes, ranging over a long time and many issue-areas, where one decision does not mean as much as the totality of the interaction process. This is the type most common in the Nordic processes.

In most cases, an actor cannot afford to stop a decision favored by the other participants as he could then easily be isolated and charged with violating the common code of compromise and obstructing the cooperation effort. Such a strategy could have harmful effects in other areas at other times, when the actor is bidding for the cooperation of the other participants. A recent example of this procedure was the continuous opposition by one of the Nordic countries to the growth of the Budget of the Council of Ministers during the last years. Although this actor has explicitly expressed his dissatisfaction with the decisions reached on the issue, he has not stopped them, but passively disapproved.

Very often decisions are reached among the Nordic governmental officials where some of the actors merely state that they 'have nothing against the decision', rather than giving positive support for the policy. Naturally, this norm for decision-making facilitates more policy results than the formal rule of unanimity would indicate. In the parliamentary sphere this procedure is even more explicit as the committee chairman here usually simply asks if anyone disapproves of a given decision before he finalizes it. If no opposition is expressed, the decision stands with or without the actual support of all the delegates.

The weakness with decisions taken in this manner is that sometimes there is no active support for their implementation. Although the policy might have a solid formal backing from all the participants, this approval does not always mean that the decision will result in immediate action. In the past, some decisions taken in these joint policy-making sessions

64

were not carried out as there was no national actor strongly in favor of their implementation. The creation of permanent staffs of Nordic officials, who are exclusively concerned with following Nordic issues on a continuous basis, seems very important here. Now, joint decisions that are taken without much actual active support can be pushed ahead by the Nordic staff. Thus half-hearted commitments by national officials and ministers will in the future have more serious implications than before. It seems that the prevailing norm of decision by the lack of active dissent in combination with a permanent staff of Nordic officials would make for considerable policy results.

In some cases, when strong differences of opinion arise among the parliamentarians in the Nordic Council a minority view can be presented together with the majority decision. In those instances, formal voting must take place to determine the actual support of a given proposal. Similar situations could not appear in the ministerial sphere as here votes are of no significance on substantive issues. However, in both the parliamentary and ministerial spheres voting is the clear exception which is to be avoided. In fact, the fear of bringing conflict of interest into the open sometimes results in the watering down of solutions. In order to avoid disagreement, a compromise position is worked out that at times have very little substance left to it. Again, we should emphasize that this tendency is probably less a function of inter-regional conflict and lack of commitment, and more a reflection on the policy-making culture in the Nordic societies, which generally disapproves of open conflict and disagreement.

We see that in many respects the norms for interaction and decision in the joint sphere are reflections of the basic elite culture regulating the national policy-making processes. The ideas of compromise, informality, technical deliberations, and consensus formation are all found in the domestic political systems in the region and are by no means unique to the cooperation efforts. In the same way as these norms have made for a gradual and harmonious social and political change in the Nordic countries, they contribute to the undramatic, incremental, stable, and piecemeal cooperation among the countries. In comparison with other regional efforts, the process might seem unexciting less than productive, and possibly without impact on the societies involved. However, one should keep in mind that the style of cooperation used is not to be confused with the actual results of

65

these efforts. If so, one would also have to question the utility of these norms for the management of domestic policy inside the Nordic countries, something very few would be willing to do.

## The Dynamics of Collective Management

We have now outlined the structural framework for Nordic interactions, identified the main actors participating in them, discussed the means, forms, and frequency of such interactions and reviewed the basic norms guiding this effort. In order to analyze the management process in more detail, we shall discuss what roles the various participating actors play in this joint enterprise. To help us explore this question we will identify four roles played in a decision-making process that seem particularly useful here. [17] These are: the initiators of policy, the vetoers of decisions and even considerations of policy, the controllers of policy, and the brokers in the policy-making process.

The initiators present and promote ideas and suggestions for new policy. The vetoers consist of those actors who because of their strategic positions and effective authority can block initiatives or prevent decisions on policy. In contrast, the controllers of policy play a more passive role and mainly have a restraining or guiding influence on the policy-making process. Their views must be taken into account because of their authority, high status, or political responsibility for policy. Finally, the brokers search for common solutions and compromises among the other actors to help keep the policy-making process flowing.

We will try to relate each type of role to the regional actors involved in Nordic cooperation, i.e. the national ministers, officials, and parliamentarians, and the Nordic parliamentary and ministerial officials. By identifying the roles performed by the various actors, we can follow the policy-making process from initiative to final decision. This way, we should be able to outline the main characteristics, strengths, and weaknesses of the Nordic experiment in collective management of transnationalism. [18]

To make our discussion clearer and more specific we will treat the ministerial and parliamentary spheres as two separate decision-making systems. Naturally, they interact and overlap, but they are still distinct enough to justify their separate treatment. One important and obvious difference between the two is that the final outcome of the ministerial process generally is a governmental policy, while the parlia-

66

mentary interactions result in internal regulations, recommendations by the Nordic Council, or other efforts to influence the ministerial decision-making. In fact, the separation between the two spheres has been more marked during the last years than before.

At the time of the establishment of the Nordic Council in 1952, it was seen as important by the founders to include the national ministers and officials in the proceedings of the Council to make its recommendations realistic and generally ensure ministerial coopera- tion in their implementation. At that time, the major legislative work of the Council was done during the short annual sessions, where the national officials would participate in the committee meetings and have an impact on decisions. Through the years, the committee work has spread throughout the year and the attendance by the national officials or ministers has become sparse. As a result, the parliamentary system of decision-making has become more separated from the national administrations and the ministerial decision-making process.

Today it is more accurate to talk about a dialogue between the members of the ministerial and parliamentary systems than an effective joint decision-making system. In particular, the Council of Ministers today advocates this practice, which in many respects excludes parlia- mentary participation from its internal cooperation process. The Nordic Council, in contrast, has recently realized the consequences of this development, partly brought on by its own efforts, and now pushes for the reinstatement of one joint regional decision-making system including both parliamentary and ministerial spheres.

It is interesting that the strongest advocates of this question in the Nordic Council are the officials of the organization. The civil servants see a serious threat to their position within the region and to their organ as a whole.[19] The parliamentarians themselves are often far more sympathetic than their staffs to the views of the ministers in this regard. Similarly, the national and Nordic officials in the ministerial sphere are more concerned about making a clear distinction between the two systems than are the ministers themselves. Apparently, the politicians involved in the cooperation process see less of a problem here as they often participate at both levels, some- times as parliamentarians and sometimes as ministers. The present debate on the question takes on a familiar tone of inter-bureaucratic rivalry over influence, access to resources, and status. From this short narration it seems that it might be analytically most useful to deal with each decision-making system separately.

Initiatives for new policy in the parliamentary sphere are generally taken by the Secretaries General, or through them by some outside group such as the Norden Associations. In a formal sense, the parliamentarians themselves initiate proposals in the Nordic Council but in reality nearly all of these originate in the secretariats. During recent years a new element has been introduced by the formation of somewhat more cohesive regional party groupings among the parliamentarians. In some cases new initiatives have originated and been developed in these party groups where the joint party secretary has played a major role. However, an indication of the central position of the national Secretaries General is that even in the case of clear party proposals, these have at times been drafted by the officials of the Nordic Council to fit the aims of the particular party group. Obviously, these officials have a considerable impact on which proposals will and will not be initiated.

The parliamentary members of the Council serve as controllers of the decision-making process. Due to their formal authority and ultimate decision-making power, their views must be taken into consideration by the initiators. Generally, the parliamentarians do not interfere with routine decisions by the staff and they almost always follow the advice and recommendations of their Secretaries General. However, these officials must be aware of the basic attitudes and views of the parliamentarians on each issue and know the limits within which they can operate.

It is interesting that in the meetings of the Standing Committees the staff of the Council is as active in the discussions and deliberations as the parliamentary delegates themselves. In many cases their opinions and comments are also listened to with greater respect than those of many parliamentarians. In four committee meetings during the fall of 1974, the 53 participating parliamentary delegates together made a total of 152 statements, about three comments per member. [20] The four attending Secretaries General and the Presidium Secretary together made 147 statements, of which the Presidium Secreatry alone accounted for 61. The four national officials each made an average of 21 statements. [21] It should be noted that these figures overemphasized the scope of the

68

parliamentary contribution, as a few delegates participated in a lively fashion while the majority had little or nothing to contribute to the discussions. We find that the intensity of participation is much higher among the officials of the Council than among its members. Except for the chairmen, the latter mainly play the role of controllers of the decision-making process, often not taking a very active part in it.

Due to the central role of the Secretaries of the Nordic Council, they also play the part of vetoers in the decision-making process. Not only can they veto ideas or proposals at the initiatory stage but throughout the process they can exercise a great restraining influence based on their superior technical knowledge, information, and prestige. It is probably fair to say that the national delegates will very rarely support an idea that is opposed by their Secretary General. The case of the recent suggestion to move all the committee secretaries to the Presidium Secretariat in Stockholm is a case in point. The Danish Secretary General has long opposed such a change. Consequently, the entire Danish delegation has refused to support it.[22]

The secreatries of the Standing Committees serve as the brokers in the decision-making process. These officials have far less authority and prestige than the Secretaries General and the Presidium Secretary, but have an important impact on the outcomes by virtue of their technical expertise within their functional areas and their roles as drafters of all committee resolutions. They do not generally take a very active part in the discussions in the committees but make their contribution in the draft proposals presented to the committee. Here the aim must be to draft a paper most likely to be accepted by all the factions of the committee to create a consensus on its acceptance. In particular, the views of the Secretaries must be taken into account as these tend to set the standards for the parliamentarians. Naturally, the committee secretaries have an opportunity to include their own views in the drafts as well to have an impact on the final result.

We can conclude that in the parliamentary sphere the roles of initiator, vetoer, and broker are all played by the civil servants of the Council, while the parliamentary delegates themselves mainly act as controllers of the decision-making process. As a result, their real influence on most issues can not be said to be very great, when compared to the impact of the officials serving them. Clearly, the Nordic officials play a very large and independent role in this system of interaction.

There is no single source of initiative in the ministerial system of Nordic cooperation. Many initiatives come from outside the system, from the Nordic Council in the form of recommendations. At other times, the initiatory role is performed by national officials working in various governmental agencies, who might respond to domestic demands. During recent years, an important part has been played by the Nordic officials. One of their major tasks has been to formulate action programs in various areas to direct the cooperation effort during the next years. In fact, according to the Statutes regulating the work on the two ministerial secretariats, one of their major functions is to take initiatives for new cooperation schemes. However, their role in this respect has not been as prominent as the one played by the Nordic parliamentary officials.

In practice, it is very difficult to trace the initiators of ministerial policy, as many actors are involved at this stage. Probably, the single most important source through the years has been the Nordic Council, i.e. the Nordic parliamentary officials. It is possible that the newly established ministerial secretariats will take over much of this role from the parliamentary sphere as their resources and experiences mature. In particular, one could expect the highly competent and well staffed ministerial secretariats to initiate more realistic, well thought out, and practical ideas than have often been presented by the Nordic Council. As more of the coordination and planning functions are transferred to the two secretariats it is also likely that the initiatives from the national organs will diminish.

In a formal sense, the Nordic officials have an additional initiatory role as they make up and present the items on the agenda of the ministerial committee meetings. In this respect, the secretariats have a valuable source of initiative vis-a-vis the national officials, who mainly respond to the issues presented by the Nordic officials.

The national officials, making up the numerous Permanent Committees of High Officials, play the part of vetoers of policy proposals. For example, the Oslo Secretariat is supposed to be closely supervised by the Permanent Committees. These should direct the work of the Secretariat and decide the tasks it should

work on. In addition, investigations or studies for new policy proposals which are initiated by the Secretariat itself should be presented
to the Permanent Committee at an early stage for its decision on the
continuation of the project. Obviously, the Nordic Secretariats have
very little flexibility in their own activities against the Permanent
Committees.

Another important source of veto is the regulation that all
proposals to the Council of Ministers must first be handled in the
appropriate committee. Thus, the national officials can very effectively withhold items from the agendas of the ministers if they
disapprove of them. One possibility for the Nordic officials is then
to try to reach the ministers directly or through pressure from the
parliamentary sphere.

In a sense, the Nordic officials in the ministerial sphere can
often find their best allies among the officials of the Nordic Council.
The possibilities for coordination and common strategies against the
vetoers in the national administrations are obvious; but, for various
reasons they have not yet been fully explored. One major reason is
that the Executive Heads of the two ministerial secretariats must be
very careful not to be too obvious in opposition to their employers
in the Permanent Committees. Such an approach would cause more
resentment and mistrust than policy results. It is the general impression
that the Cultural Secretariat has more independence from its Committee
than does the Oslo Secretariat. One reason for this difference is the
non-controversial, often technical nature of the questions handled in
Copenhagen in contrast to the often highly politicized issues in Oslo. [23]

The national ministers play the role of controllers of the
decision-making process. Due to their heavy domestic workload they
can not devote much time and effort to most Nordic issues. Rather,
they must depend on their subordinates, the national officials, to
interpret and represent their views on most questions. As they are
the ultimate decision-makers on all questions of policy, their views
naturally must be taken into account by the other actors. The
national officials have numerous opportunities through daily contacts with their ministers to check their positions and get formal
clearance for a policy stand.

Naturally, the most politicized and important issues come to
the direct attention of the ministers themselves in their periodic

71

meetings. In fact, compared to other inter-governmental efforts it is surprising how many issues are brought up to this level of decision. On many seemingly minor questions, the ministers not only make the formal decision, but also discuss and deliberate the question among themselves. One fairly unique feature of the Nordic cooperation process is also the ability of the national representatives to make many decisions directly at the table on the basis of the preceding discussion. However, on the whole the ministers must depend on their staff for information on available alternatives as well as for policy suggestions. Therefore, their role is more that of a controller of the decision-making process than that of a direct vetoer immediately prohibiting further deliberations.

The newly established joint Nordic Secretariats play the role of brokers in the ministerial sphere of policy-making. Before their creation the ministerial sphere lacked actors that could work independently to reach consensus and agreement among the five national governments. In those days, the Nordic parliamentary officials partly played this role also in the ministerial sphere. However, their aim was more to penetrate each national administration with Nordic ideas, views, and solutions, than to work toward an agreement among the governments.

The Nordic Ministerial Secretariats serve the same function as the secretaries of the committees of the Nordic Council, in that they draft proposals for policy statements, reports, programs, etc. However, these drafts are usually given much closer examination by the national delegates than the parliamentarians can provide. One reason for this is that in the ministerial sphere the national representatives are the experts, aided by large staffs of specialists in the area. In contrast, the parliamentarians and the Secretaries General are far less specialists in each question than the committee secretary himself.

A recent example can be offered of the close scrutiny with which the Permanent Committees examine the draft proposals of the Secretariats. In 1974 the Nordic Cultural Secretariat prepared a program for continued Nordic cultural cooperation. In the introduction to this policy statement a paragraph dealt with the goals of Nordic cultural cooperation.[24] Here we can note some interesting differences between the draft, written by the Secretariat in September, and the final version approved by the Council of Ministers in December 1974.

Draft Version (September)
>Throughout this program there is an ambition to strengthen
>Nordic cohesion and the value of a Nordic cultural policy
>for its own sake. Many measures taken have a national
>motive, as it is in the interest of each country to cooperate
>with other Nordic countries to achieve better national
>results, but at the same time, the actions of the Nordic
>countries are still aimed at fulfilling the goals of the Nordic
>Cultural Treaty and transmitting and developing the common
>Nordic cultural heritage.

Final Version (December)
>Throughout this program there is an ambition to fulfill
>the goals of the Nordic Cultural Treaty to further develop
>the Nordic cultural heritage and then also contribute to
>the construction of a joint Nordic cultural policy.

One sees quite clearly in these two paragraphs how the effort by the Nordic Secretariat to stress the integrative, Nordic value of cultural cooperation has been watered down considerably by the national representatives. The latter did not accept the implicit critique of their motives for taking part in joint ventures but settled for a very general statement of their ambitions in this area. Thus, the officials of the Nordic ministerial secretariats have less opportunity to include their own views than have the parliamentary officials. Formulations that go beyond the acceptable limits are easily noted and changed or omitted in the Permanent Committees.

The technique of linking issues to reach package deals of acceptable solutions has not been used much in the Nordic region. One reason for this has been the decentralized nature of the cooperation process. Each Permanent Committee handles its own functional area independently of the work of the other. Since the creation of a coordinating Committee of Deputies, the possibilities for far-reaching compromises linking several issue-areas seem more likely. However, these solutions are more likely to be reached at the political level of the ministers than at the level of the national officials, who carefully guard their particular domain.[25] Due to these factors, the joint Secretariats can only play a limited broker role in the decision-making process. Their impact on the outcomes seem considerably less than that of the parliamentary officials in this regard.

We have seen how the initiator and broker roles are played by the Nordic ministerial officials, the veto role by the national officials and the controller role by the ministers themselves. It is clear that the independence and impact of the Nordic officials on the decision-making process is considerably less in this system than in the parliamentary system of operation. However, while the Secretaries General of the Nordic Council have more than twenty years of experience and tradition to fall back on, the recently established ministerial secretariats have not yet fully found their place in the system. It is quite possible that over the years these secretariats will get to play a more decisive role as well, if they gain the trust of the national officials and ministers and acquire forceful leaderships. Already, there are indications that the central role of the secretariats in collective budgeting has enhanced their impact on regional policies. The joint Nordic appropriations are scrutinized by the secretariats which then have an opportunity to emphasize particularly desired projects.

If we look at the total Nordic decision-making system, including both the parliamentary and ministerial spheres, we find a rather complex net of interactions, roles, and processes. The Nordic Council system in total plays the major initiatory role in this policy-making system. The controllers are the politicians, parliamentarians and ministers, who oversee the broad workings of the cooperation process and personally get involved only in politicized issues. The basically similar positions and interests of the politicians are often distorted and separated by their dependence on various groups of officials for information and advice. The tradition of informal meetings with ministers and parliamentarians without the presence of any civil servants is useful to bring them together as politicians without the restraining effect of official role playing.

The vetoers of joint Nordic policy are found in the national administrations. It is natural that these actors can block the joint decision-making process since they are the actors who implement and enforce the joint policy nationally. Therefore, it is particularly important to get the support of these officials in the initial stages of the policy-making effort. At times a political decision is needed to enlist the support of this group but generally it is perceptive to sensible and practical proposals that do not gravely threaten its interests.

TABLE 3:5

POLICY-MAKING ROLES OF REGIONAL ACTORS

| Actor | Roles | | | |
|---|---|---|---|---|
| | Initiator | Vetoer | Controller | Broker |
| Parliamentary Sphere | | | | |
| National Parliamentarians | | | X | |
| Secretaries General | X | X | | |
| Committee Secretaries | | | | X |
| Ministerial Sphere | | | | |
| National Ministers | | | X | |
| National Officials | | X | | |
| Nordic Ministerial Officials | X | | | X |
| Total Policy-Making System | | | | |
| National Ministers | | | X | |
| National Parliamentarians | X | | X | |
| National Officials | | X | | |
| Nordic Parliamentary Officials | X | | | |
| Nordic Ministeral Officials | | | | X |

ˌ It must be underscored that these officials are only marginally concerned with Nordic issues as their basic orientation is toward solving immediate national problems. We see in Table 3:6 that almost half of the responding civil servants devote less than 10 per cent of their work to Nordic cooperation issues. This figure is particularly interesting when we consider that our questionnaire was only sent to those officials identified as working with Nordic questions. We also note that a few officials, notably in Sweden and Denmark, spend more than 50 per cent of their time on Nordic affairs. These figures indicate the greater administrative resources devoted to Nordic cooperation in these two countries. Here special offices for Nordic coordination have been established to assist the representatives in the Committee of Deputies. However, these offices do not handle the cooperation schemes for each functional area. Rather, one characteristic feature of the Nordic process is that it reaches into the national administrations at all levels.

TABLE 3:6

PERCENTAGE OF WORKLOAD DEVOTED TO NORDIC COOPERATION AFFAIRS

Percentage of Yearly Workload Devoted to Nordic Issues

| Actor | Less Than 10% N | % | 10-15% N | % | 15-25% N | % | 25-50% N | % | More Than 50% N | % | Total N | % |
|---|---|---|---|---|---|---|---|---|---|---|---|---|
| National Officials | 23 | 44 | 11 | 21 | 9 | 17 | 3 | 6 | 6 | 12 | 52 | 100 |
| Parliamentarians | 24 | 67 | 9 | 25 | 2 | 6 | 1 | 3 | 0 | 0 | 36 | 100 |
| National Actors | 47 | 53 | 20 | 23 | 11 | 13 | 4 | 5 | 6 | 7 | 88 | 100 |

Question: How large a part of your yearly workload do you devote to Nordic issues?

Source: Mail Questionnaire to National Actors, fall 1974.

The system is horizontally decentralized by the involvement of virtually all governmental agencies and vertically decentralized by the participation of central ministries, autonomous agencies, local authorities, ministers, state secretaries, and low level officials. Thus, if we want to view "international organizations according to how far they involve the effective policy-making processes of governments rather than how independent they have become," [26] we find that the Nordic process reaches deeply into the national administrations but rarely occupies a major part of the officials' attention. However, it is more important that the Nordic aspect has become routine for many national officials in their daily work. In many respects, the Nordic issues are not treated as one specific type of issue, but are handled as one dimension of most policy problems facing the official. Thus, the Nordic aspect is fairly well integrated into the national policy processes.

In this system of "multi-bureaucratic decision-making", the Nordic officials serve as brokers and objective promoters of joint solutions. The national control of the activities of the two ministerial Secretariats is fairly tight making them service organs of the trans-governmental process instead of independent and forceful Nordic institutions.

\* \* \* \* \* \* \* \* \* \* \* \* \* \* \* \* \*

We have observed the existence of a network of elite interactions in the Nordic region that makes for a joint decision-making process. This joint process of coordination, consultation, and decision is fairly decentralized, taking place across many functional areas and at all levels of government. Rather than functioning above the national level in a traditional regional manner, the process reaches across the national administrations, parliaments, and ministries to create a trans-governmental interaction pattern. The interactions are intensive enough to maintain a continuous process of collective management and at the same time decentralized enough to reach deeply into the national decision-making structures. As a result, policy solutions can be presented that are nationally acceptable and implemented and yet have a common Nordic basis. The role of the Nordic institutions is mainly to support this interaction pattern and to facilitate the output of collective remedies to national problems.

77

# 4. Achievements and Failures

In order to evaluate the relative success of the North European effort of collective management, one must analyze the policy product emerging from this joint process. Hopefully, the elaborate institutional framework and intensive elite interactions discussed in the preceding chapter result in the coordination and harmonization of national policy over a broad range of issue-areas. If so, one can argue that the North European experiment of collective management is successful. If this is not occurring, however, it would seem the management techniques developed are weak or inadequate to foster joint policy products directed at improving societal control. In either case, valuable lessons oan be learned from the Nordic example.

Our discussion here cannot go into great detail in every policy sector or hope to analyze each policy output resulting from Nordic processes. Such a description of the Nordic policy achievements. has been made by other writers elsewhere. [1] Rather, we are trying to draw the rough profile of joint policy, indicating in what issue-areas the Nordic efforts have proven more or less productive. To aid us in this task, we shall use the widely adopted Lindberg list of policy areas.[2] This list of 22 different governmental functions was constructed for the analysis of the scope of collective policy in the EC. For that reason, the list overemphasizes the economic functions of government (12 out of 22 areas) at the expense of the other areas of policy. This bias in the list should be kept in mind when we use it in the Nordic case.

## External Relations Functions

The Nordic region is split in its formal approach to national security. After the failure of the effort to create a Scandinavian

TABLE 4:1

## THE LINDBERG LIST OF ISSUE-AREAS

External Relations Functions

1. Military Security
2. Diplomatic influence and participation in world affairs
3. Economic and military aid to other polities
4. Commercial relations with other polities

Political-Constitutional Functions

5. Public health and safety and maintenance of order
6. Political participation
7. Access to legal-normative system

Social-Cultural Functions

8. Cultural and recreational affairs
9. Education and research
10. Social welfare policies

Economic Functions

11. Counter-cyclical policy
12. Regulation of economic competition and other government controls on prices and investments
13. Agricultural protection
14. Economic development and planning
15. Exploitation and protection of natural resources
16. Regulation and support of transportation
17. Regulation and support of mass-media of communication
18. Labor-management relations
19. Fiscal policy
20. Balance of payments stability
21. Domestic monetary policy
22. Assurance of free movement of goods, services, and other factors of production.

From Leon Lindberg and Stuart Scheingold, Europe's Would Be Polity (Englewood Cliffs: Prentice-Hall, 1970), p. 60.

Defense Alliance in 1948-49 by Denmark, Norway, and Sweden, three types of security policy can be found in the region. Iceland, Denmark, and Norway are NATO-allies, Sweden is an armed non-aligned nation, while Finland is nonaligned with a special understanding with the Soviet Union. Obviously, security questions can not be handled jointly in the region, at least not in a formal sense. On the other hand, if one accepts the notion of a "Nordic balance", one must also face the question whether there is a factual policy coordination among the Nordic countries in this policy area.[3]

The idea has been advanced that the Nordic countries engage in negative policy coordination in security policy by adhering to this strategic theory of a Nordic balance. Although not identical in contents, the national security arrangements are mutually supportive and strengthen each other, according to this line of thought. For example, the Danish and Norwegian "no base" policy with regard to NATO is aimed at lessening the pressure on Sweden and Finland, the Swedish policy of armed non-alliance is partially a result of consideration for the Finnish position, and the possibilities for Finland to stay fairly independent of the Soviet Union are closely dependent on the positions of the other Nordic countries. Thus, in spite of the formally different security policies in the region, there actually seems to exist a certain degree of joint policy in this area. The crucial question here is, if and to what extent the national governments deliberately and consciously coordinate their policies in accordance with this theory. Possibly, these mutually supportive security arrangments have come about without actual joint decision-making, consultation, or consideration.

Unfortunately, the Nordic governments would have very little interest in showing that a joint policy-making process takes place in this area, if in fact it does. Therefore, it is very hard to determine empirically if these seemingly negatively coordinated policies are the result of joint processes or merely the fortunate outcomes of non-deliberate developments. All we know is that the Nordic Defense Ministers and various officials in their agencies meet on a continuous basis to discuss questions of mutual interest. Quite probably, an intense exchange of information also takes place between the Nordic NATO members and Sweden. Thus, the potential for a joint policy-making process exists in this area of policy . However, we must finally emphasize that the formal security arrangements are quite distinct and dissimilar, a fact that is often stressed by the Nordic governments themselves.

The formal split in security policy has not hampered an intensive effort to coordinate foreign policy in issue-areas other than security, to increase the region's diplomatic influence and participation in world affairs. Being five small countries without great individual leverage in world politics, most of their global foreign policy has been directed through multilateral forums. Here, the tradition of joint Nordic appearances, voting, and delegations is firmly established. In global politics the countries have managed to go beyond mere consultations and exchanges of information to act frequently as a unit in many international conferences and assemblies.

In multilateral diplomacy, the Nordic group is characterized by the phenomenon of "externalization" described by several integration theorists. Phillipe Schmitter, among others, has argued that one crucial aspect of an integration process is the ability to increasingly act as one unit toward the surrounding world.[4] Ernst Haas and E.T. Rowe have empirically tested the amount of "externalization" for a number of regional organizations.[5] They used voting cohesion in the General Assembly of the United Nations as an indicator of regional externalization. Haas-Rowe found that the Nordic group is more cohesive than the EC countries, and that it is one of the few Western groups that can show a continuous increase in group cohesion during the last twenty years. A number of other studies of UN roll calls have also pointed to the high voting cohesion within the Nordic group during the post-war period.[6] These aspects of Nordic externalization in the United Nations are combined with similar joint activities in other international organizations, such as UNESCO, IMF, UNCTAD, GATT, and ILO.

In contrast, bilateral relations have generally been harder to coordinate. For several years, consular officers of the Nordic countries have been instructed to assist citizens of other Nordic countries if they lack consular representation in the area. Beyond this consular cooperation, it is only recently, and with mixed success, that some positive coordination such as recognition of new states or governments has been achieved on the bilateral level. However, one should remember that although the countries in many cases act separately and sometimes seemingly in conflict with each other, they almost always consult and inform each other before any such move. Thus, the neighbors are informed and aware of the steps to be taken by one of the countries, although they might not always agree with the action.

Economic aid or development assistance has, since 1962, been coordinated to some extent. At this time a joint committee was established to coordinate the regional aid most efficiently. Several joint projects have been undertaken, such as in Tanzania (since 1963) and Kenya (since 1967). About 50 million dollars has been devoted to these joint projects. In addition to these projects, there is joint Nordic representation in the World Bank and the African and Asian Development Banks. Currently, a joint project in Bangladesh is being contemplated.[7] However, during recent years the various national aid organizations have come to prefer joint coordination and harmonization of projects and activities rather than jointly executed projects. Several practical difficulties have hampered the effectiveness of the joint projects that have outweighed the symbolic value of a joint appearance. As the purpose of the coordination of policy is to achieve the most efficient use of regional resources for development assistance, it has been argued that continuous coordination, consultation, and harmonization of development policies can be more profitable than the often complicated task of setting up and administering joint projects. The Nordic countries do not give military aid, although they sell arms on a limited basis.

With regard to commercial relations with other polities, the Nordic record is mixed. On the one hand, a common front towards the Common Market has been lacking ever since its creation. On the other hand, the Nordic countries, except Iceland, managed to agree on a joint negotiator, Nils Montan, and a joint position in the concluding sessions of the GATT negotiations in 1967. Due to this united front in the Kennedy-Round, the countries managed to get very favorable terms, mainly from the EC, and also to be included in the select meetings of the larger trading nations. Today, continuous consultations and discussions take place among the countries to try a somewhat similar effort at the ongoing GATT negotiations. This time Denmark can.not be formally included in the Nordic delegation in Geneva, although it participates in the preparatory meetings with the Nordic group as before. Instead, its first commitment is to the Common Market.

On the whole, however, each nation directs its own commercial relations and the intensity of joint policy does not generally go beyond consultation, discussion, and negative coordination. This was the case, for example, in the countries' negotiations with the EC in 1970-1973 to reach commercial agreements with that unit. The different economic interests, ties, and concerns of the five countries show up continuously in their commercial relations with other international actors and make positive policy coordination very difficult.

The situation has further deteriorated since 1973, when Denmark alone joined the EC. This country is now bound by the arrangements worked out inside this organization and can only consider Nordic alternatives within that framework. In contrast, it has been argued that Denmark has a valuable role to play as a bridge between the Nordic and EC groupings. By being represented in the EC councils she can present Nordic positions and indirectly help the other countries get a favorable hearing by the EC. According to this way of reasoning, her membership has not weakened the chances for Nordic policy coordination but in fact strengthened the Nordic position in European forums. As a means to show her continued Nordic solidarity, the Danish government allows the other Nordic governments free access to internal EC documents and proposals sent to Copenhagen. She could be regarded as a Nordic fifth column operating inside foreign territory. This argument also improves the Danish bargaining position in Brussels, as she can claim to speak for not only herself but for the entire Nordic region of 22 million people. So, the idea of bridge-building might have been constructed more as a means to improve the Danish situation in the EC and less as an attempt to stress continued Nordic solidarity.[8]

## Political-Constitutional Functions

There is intensive Nordic policy coordination in the area of public health and safety and the maintenance of order. The officials of the national health agencies have met regularly since 1929 to coordinate their activities. There is a common labor market for most types of medical personnel, standardization and testing of pharmaceutical products take place, medical prescriptions can be filled by pharmacists in any of the countries, persons visiting another Nordic country can get hospital care on the same basis as the nationals, there is a Nordic School of Public Health for specialized training, and efforts are made to coordinate medical and social statistics in the region. In border districts local services, such as doctors, ambulances, fire departments, etc., are extended across the national borders to save resources and give better regional service. Since 1974, a Nordic Treaty on the Protection of the Environment gives citizens in any Nordic country the same legal protection from harmful pollution or industrial waste as the citizens of the country that is the source of the potential danger.

Continuous cooperation takes place between the police and court authorities to give equal treatment to all Nordic citizens and facilitate regional public order. For example, criminal records in one country can be requested by another country's police department or criminal court. The rules of extradition are similar. A court in one country can, under certain conditions, sentence a person for crimes committed in another Nordic country. A sentenced person can, under certain conditions, serve his term, pay his fine, etc., in a Nordic country other than that in which the crime was committed. A rule requiring persons to act as witnesses not only in their own courts but in any Nordic trial has recently been enacted. Persons ordered by a court to pay alimony or child support can not avoid this expense by moving to another Nordic country, as these rules have been jointly enforced since 1931. Driver's licenses are directly interchangeable between countries without having to submit to any tests. Obviously, numerous efforts take place to equalize the conditions of health, safety, and order in the region. This has been particularly needed as the increased mobility of people has required coordination and harmonization of policy to ensure equal treatment of all Nordic citizens regardless of their temporary location.

The rules governing the rights to political participation are very restrictive in most nations. In principle, only citizens of a country have the privilege of voting, holding office, being a public employee, etc. This has also been the case in the Nordic countries. For example, the civil services are basically closed to nationals of any other Nordic country. In recent years, a problem has arisen as the large Finnish population in Sweden not only has been unable to participate in Swedish elections but sometimes also lost their right to vote in their home country. Since 1971, new rules have been enacted in Finland making it possible for Finnish migrants in Sweden to keep their vote at home.

During recent years, the question of extending voting rights in local elections to Nordic citizens residing in another country has been discussed. The Swedish government has been the most active, responding to a demand from the large Finnish population living in Sweden. At first, an effort was made to find a joint Nordic solution by enacting similar provisions in all the Nordic countries. However, due to internal pressures, the Swedish government acted ahead of the other countries and decided to give voting and office holding privileges in local elections not only to Nordic but to all immigrants residing in the country. As a result, the Nordic aspect of the new rule was basically taken away, as Nordic citizens would not be treated differently from any other immigrant groups. In contrast, the other countries kept the Nordic preference and now extend voting privileges in local elections to all Nordic citizens residing in the community.

Efforts at joint policy in the area of legal-normative rules have a long tradition in the Nordic region. Meetings of Nordic jurists began in 1872. As a result of this long history of uniform law making, the Nordic countries have come very far in this area, further, for example, than the EC and perhaps even the states of the U.S. While the technique used before the Second World War was mainly one of joint committees of legal authorities making identical laws, the most common present approach is that of parallel national committees that consult and coordinate their work and timing. As the making and changing of laws have become a highly politicized process, the slow and basically nonpolitical method of acting through Nordic committees of jurists is not very practical. Instead, an effort is now made to coordinate the investigatory work, writing, proposing, and final enacting of Nordic laws to ensure a joint effect of the national laws.

Basically, all areas of law making are included in this process of creating uniform Nordic laws. They are, for example, constitutional law, family law, civil law, criminal law, process law, administrative law, business law, tax law, and international law. A detailed description of each of the many hundred rules and norms passed through the years after a joint Nordic policy process would be too extensive for this study. Instead we will demonstrate how the enactment of these uniform laws has shifted over time. Thus, we can provide statistics on the number of national laws that were the product of joint Nordic coordination.

86

TABLE 4:2

UNIFORM NATIONAL LAWS ORIGINATING FROM NORDIC COOPERATION  –1975
(Excluding social welfare legislation)

| Time Period | Denmark | Finland | Iceland | Norway | Sweden | Total | National | Laws |
|---|---|---|---|---|---|---|---|---|
| | N | N | N | N | N | N | % | % |
| -1919 | 15 | 1 | 8 | 16 | 13 | 53 | 11 | – |
| 1920-1945 | 25 | 18 | 14 | 24 | 35 | 96 | 19 | – |
| 1946-1950 | 4 | 4 | 0 | 2 | 3 | 13 | 3 | 4 |
| 1951-1955 | 3 | 2 | 2 | 4 | 6 | 17 | 4 | 5 |
| 1956-1960 | 10 | 4 | 0 | 8 | 16 | 38 | 8 | 12 |
| 1961-1965 | 18 | 12 | 10 | 16 | 12 | 68 | 14 | 20 |
| 1966-1970 | 15 | 14 | 2 | 17 | 22 | 70 | 15 | 21 |
| 1971-1975 | 23 | 23 | 7 | 25 | 46 | 124 | 26 | 38 |
| Total: | | | | | | | | |
| -1975 | 113 | 78 | 43 | 112 | 163 | 479 | 100 | – |
| 1946-1975 | 73 | 59 | 21 | 72 | 115 | 330 | – | 100 |

Source: Nordic Council, Oversikt over det nordiska lovsamarbeides utvikling og resultater, Nordisk Utredningsserie 1976:32 (Stockholm: Nordic Council, 1977).

87

We see in Table 4:2 that the making of uniform laws has a long tradition in the Nordic region. Almost one-third of all national laws created by joint Nordic coordination processes through 1975 were enacted before 1946. We also note that while the number of new laws was low and stable following the Second World War, by the late 1950s there was a marked increase in output. In particular, the last five years covered, 1971-1975, have seen the steady flow of new uniform laws. In fact, almost 80 percent of all uniform laws enacted since the Second World War have been passed since 1960.

## Social-Cultural Functions

One of the corner-stones of Nordic cooperation has been the cultural sphere. Due to the great original cultural homogeneity of the region, continuous cultural influences from outside the area, and a conscious desire to keep the Nordic culture intact in spite of these external influences, the political leaders in the countries have regarded the cultural sphere as a very important aspect of Nordic cooperation. Also, joint cultural policy has often come more easily, been less controversial, less threatening to national interests, and has sometimes served as a substitute for failures in other policy areas.

When discussing Nordic cultural cooperation one should keep in mind that this concept is rather broadly defined in this region. It does not refer only to cooperation in the area of literature, art, music, etc., but a substantial part of Nordic cultural cooperation concerns the policy areas of education and research. For that reason, we must discuss these two policy areas together as they are very closely connected in the Nordic region.

We have already discussed the rather comprehensive institutional framework within which joint cultural policies are formed. In particular, since the Nordic Cultural Treaty became effective on January 1, 1972, much policy making has been handled through joint processes. In 1974, 31.8 million Danish Kroner ($6 million) was devoted to various cultural projects in the Nordic Cultural Budget (this figure excludes the costs for the administration of the Cultural Secretariat). Of this sum, 45 percent went to research, 23 percent to education, and 32 percent to cultural projects in general.[9] Almost all of the funds spent on research are allocated to the fourteen permanent Nordic research institutes while over two-thirds of the money for education goes to the eight joint institutions in this area. In contrast, the funds for activities in the strictly cultural sphere are mainly spent on projects, programs, and activities of a non-institutional character.

Let us briefly examine what type of activities are undertaken in the area of Nordic cultural cooperation. [10] Cooperation and coordination among scientists in virtually every field take place either in permanent institutes, cooperation committees, or specific projects. Joint publications are very common, in fact, over eighty Nordic scientific periodicals appear regularly. [11] Higher education is pooled in many areas, where particular specialization or expensive equipment is required. An effort has been made to harmonize education from the primary to the university levels. For example, students should be able to move freely within the Nordic area and still be able to continue their education without loss of credits, financial benefits, or facing new requirements. This harmonization process has been most successful at the primary and secondary levels and is kept up as a continuous process. In recent years, a program for adult education has been initiated. Courses in the history, culture, and language of the other Nordic countries have been encouraged at all levels.

The recreation of a joint Nordic book-market has been encouraged by support for translations, a Nordic Literary Prize, abolition of duties on books, etc. Cooperation in music, art, film, and theatre also takes place to enrich the cultural life in the region. Radio and TV are used to promote cultural exchanges through joint programs. Finally, numerous cultural funds, societies, and groups exist that work for a Nordic culture at the grass-roots level. Many of these voluntary organizations are funded by public means. The remote location of Iceland and the Faeroe Islands has encouraged the establishment of a Nordic House in Reykjavik and a Cultural Center in Torshavn, both financed through the Nordic Cultural Budget.

Obviously, the policy areas of culture, education, and research are to a large extent handled jointly. It is true that the success here can in part be explained by the non-controversial nature of the policy area. But it is also noticeable that the effect of these policies reaches far into the domestic structures and societies and may have important integrative consequences for the region.

The Nordic countries are well-known for their extensive social welfare policies, guaranteeing the well-being of the residents from the "cradle to the grave." It is therefore no surprise that substantial efforts have been made to extend these policies to the regional level as well. The Ministers of Social Policy started regular meetings to discuss joint policy as early as 1926. The thrust of these efforts of cooperation has not been to harmonize the national social policies per se, but rather to solve the problems facing persons moving within the Nordic region. The basic agreement regulating these aspects is the 1955 Convention on Social Security, that has been followed by several other less broad and more specific agreements for particular areas of social policy.

The fundamental principle behind those regulations is that every Nordic resident should enjoy the same social benefits regardless of where he or she is temporarily located. Thus, hospital, unemployment, old age, and accident insurance can be transferred between the countries without loss of coverage, premiums, or points accumulated. In addition, constant contact is kept between the national authorities responsible for social policy to ensure the identical implementation of these rules. Also planning, proposals, studies, and new national regulations are handled jointly to avoid differences in this area that could cause future problems. As a result of these agreements and the joint policy planning, the Nordic region is, by and large, one unit in the area of social welfare. Some national differences exist, due to various needs and means, but to the Nordic peoples the benefits enjoyed are similar wherever they desire to settle.

## Economic Functions

In the area of economic policy, the intensity of joint Nordic policy has not been as great as in many of the other policy areas. In fact, the history of the efforts towards creating a Nordic Economic Union is rather negative. Throughout the 1950s unsuccessful efforts were made, that were finally overcome by the larger European solutions of EEC and EFTA in 1959.[12]   A second scheme (NORDEK) was

90

launched in 1968, but again the Nordic option was set aside for the larger European market. [13]   The situation has been somewhat complicated since January 1973, when Denmark became a member of European Economic Community and now must adhere to the Community rules rather than the Nordic coordination whenever a conflict occurs.

In the area of counter-cyclical policy some coordination takes place to reach similar views and evaluations of the needs for measures. Regulation of economic competition and other governmental controls on prices and investments has only been handled in a joint manner on a very limited basis. Corporate taxation, interest policy, etc., vary considerably between the countries. Several provisions in this regard were proposed in the NORDEK treaty, but they never came into effect. Today, Denmark follows the extensive Community regulations in this area.

Agricultural protection has always been a difficult problem in Nordic negotiations for economic unions. While Denmark is a low price country, depending on agricultural exports, the other countries are pursuing high price policies with extensive protection of their farmers. On the whole the countries act separately in this issue-area, although  some policy discussions and exchanges take place in Nordic committees for agricultural and fishery questions.

In the area of economic development and planning, substantive results have been achieved through joint efforts. Regional planning and support is often handled in a joint Nordic perspective. Trans-border cooperation is common in areas with particular regional problems, such as the North Cap and Oresund regions. The Nordic Fund for Industrial Development supports technical schemes to increase industrial productivity. A special Development Fund for Iceland was established  in 1970, to aid that country in its development policies. In addition, substantial funds were given for the reconstruction of the Vestman Islands after the 1971 volcanic eruption and severe destruction of that island community. Finally, a Nordic Investment Bank helps draw foreign capital to the region. The Bank began operation on July 1, 1976, and has a basic capital of about $500 million and a lending capacity of just above one billion  dollars. Obviously, in this specific economic policy area the results go beyond the general trend for joint economic policy in the region.

Exploitation and protection of natural resources partly take place in a joint manner. NORDEL coordinates the production and distribution of hydroelectric energy within the region to ensure the most efficient use of the available water power. A committee for atomic energy questions meets regularly to try to coordinate policies in this area. In recent years the joint regional usage of the Norwegian oil and gas resources has been widely discussed but so far no concrete schemes have appeared. A Nordic Convention on the Protection of the Environment was signed in 1974 to set the normative guidelines for joint policies in this area. In addition, various conventions have been enacted for the protection of the Baltic Sea.

Nordic cooperation in the area of transportation has a long tradition and has produced many results. The Nordic Council has pushed for efforts in this area to ensure the free movement of goods and people in the region. Discriminatory railway practices have been abolished, the road network has been planned in conjunction with the needs of the neighboring countries, and a joint international airline (SAS) has been operating since 1947. In 1973, these efforts in cooperative transportation were formalized and further strengthened by the new Nordic Transportation Treaty which outlined directions for more intensive work in this area.

In the area of mass media and communications, joint policy is common. A postal union dates back to 1873, inter-Nordic postal rates are identical to domestic rates for many types of mail, and telephone and telegraph cooperation ensures rapid and cheap communications across borders. The national radio and TV companies cooperate extensively, among others in the NORDIVISION system, to exchange programs, pool technical resources, and share expenses. Currently, plans are made to expand the national TV networks by satellite into the neighboring countries to increase the output and reach a Nordic TV audience.

Labor-management relations are handled in very similar fashions in all countries. In chapter two we discussed the extent of coordination between the national organizations representing labor and employers. In addition, all governments take a similar approach to labor issues as the Social Democratic parties tend to dominate the political arenas.

In fiscal policy, the regional effort does not go beyond periodic interactions for consultation, discussion, and exchanges. No positive policy coordination seems to exist in this area. Balance-of-payment problems are, by and large, handled separately, although efforts are sometimes made to coordinate policies. For example, all countries have participated in the European Snake, which tie their currencies to the German D-mark. The central banks can supply each other with short-term bank credits if the need for foreign exchange arises. The countries also have one joint director of the IMF. It seems that in this issue-area the countries have managed better to coordinate their policies on the international scene than internally within the region.

The same observation is true in the area of domestic monetary policy. Between 1873 and the First World War the Scandinavian region constituted a currency union, based on the gold standard with the common unit Krona. However, since that time the monetary policies have drifted apart and today separate national systems operate. Regular consultations take place in this area, as in most others, but the difficulties of creating a joint monetary policy seem great.

The free movement of goods, services, and labor in the region is ensured by various agreements. Since 1954 a common labor market for wage earners has made possible the mobility of surplus workers to areas of labor shortage. In 1967, tariffs on industrial goods were removed, leading to a significant increase in inter-Nordic trade. Efforts have been made continuously to ease the crossing of borders. Since 1958 the region is a passport union for both Nordic and non-Nordic citizens. Joint customs stations operate along the borders to avoid double work. Customs clearance has been considerably eased for most types of crossings. It is interesting that since Denmark's entrance into the Common Market these Nordic policies to assure the free movement within the region have been kept intact. Thus, Denmark has not been cut off from its Nordic partners because of its new commitments on the Continent but serves in some respects as a bridge between the Nordic and the larger European areas.

## Policy Assessment

We have now briefly outlined the major policy achievements and failures across the 22 issue-areas defined on our list. In order to better assess in what areas the Nordic strategy has proven the most or least successful, we shall summarize our review in a table indicating

## FIGURE 4:1

### SCALE OF POLICY INTENSITY

| Intensity of Coordination: | Lack of Coordination | | Negative Coordination | | Positive Coordination |
|---|---|---|---|---|---|
| Policy Output: | Incompatible | Not Incompatible | Compatible | Mutually Supportive | Joint Output |

the intensity of policy coordination in different sectors. We will then differentiate between positive and negative policy coordination and argue that positive coordination requires a more intensive collective management effort than negative coordination. We do not argue that one type is a priori superior to the other, but merely that one type of policy output in a certain issue-area requires a more intensive policy-making process than the other. This is the case as the participants must not only avoid conflicting policies but also settle for one common solution.

We work with two variables: the scope of policy over twenty-two issue-areas, and the two types of intensity of the policy-making process in each issue-area. We can now compare the scores for each policy across the spectrum of issues. The evaluation of which type of coordination dominates each issue-area must be approximate. This is the case as the two types of policy coordination really are areas on a scale of compatibility. Here, the extreme points are easily identified, while in the grey area of "not incompatible to mutually supportive" policy it is harder to make distinctions. In spite of this weakness in the scheme used, we think the table can show the differences in scope and intensity of Nordic policy.

We find in Table 4:3 that the scope of joint Nordic policy is extremely broad covering all 22 issue-areas. This would indicate that the collective management effort tries to cope with virtually all social and economic issues facing the countries. One could say that the horizontal ambition of the North European process is great. When comparing the intensity of joint policy one notes some striking differences. While positive coordination dominates the areas of social-cultural activities and the political-constitutional functions, there is an even split between positive and negative coordination in the economic field as well as in external relations. Within the economic area we also see some differences. While some issues, such as development and planning, exploitation of natural resources, transportation, communication, and freedom of movement score high, other issues linked to economic management and control have fared less well.

Overall, the impression prevails that in questions concerned with transnational flows and the sharing of scarce resources within the region, the governments have reached far going agreements. In contrast, policies aimed at protecting each society from external

TABLE 4:3

## THE SCOPE AND INTENSITY OF JOINT NORDIC POLICY 1977

| Governmental Functions | Type of Coordination Dominant | |
|---|---|---|
| | Negative | Positive |
| External Relations: | | |
| 1. Military security | X | |
| 2. Diplomatic influence | | X |
| 3. Economic and military aid | | X |
| 4. Commercial relations | X | |
| Political-Constitutional | | |
| 5. Public health, safety, order | | X |
| 6. Political participation | X | |
| 7. Access to legal system | | X |
| Social-Cultural | | |
| 8. Cultural, recreational | | X |
| 9. Education and research | | X |
| 10. Social welfare | | X |
| Economic Funtions | | |
| 11. Counter-cyclical policy | X | |
| 12. Regulation of economic compe-tition and other controls | X | |
| 13. Agricultural protection | X | |
| 14. Development and Planning | | X |
| 15. Exploitation and protection of natural resources | | X |
| 16. Regulation and support of transportation | | X |
| 17. Regulation and support of mass-media communications | | X |
| 18. Labor-Management relations | | X |
| 19. Fiscal policy | X | |
| 20. Balance of payments | X | |
| 21. Domestic monetary policy | X | |
| 22. Assurance of free movement of goods, services, and other factors | | X |
| Total scope of issue-areas | 9 | 13 |

disturbances have been less successfully handled collectively. Here the basic national orientations of each participating unit has limited the results of collective deliberations. One could say that while "neighborhood issues" have been successfully managed in Northern Europe, "national issues" have been less successfully managed. This observation would point to a certain unwillingness by the governments to compromise their privilege to pursue national policies for short-term domestic political gain in favor of coordinated regional policies which might in fact prove more effective in the long-run. This is not to say that significant results have not been accomplished in this region in terms of the production of joint policy. Most likely, the overall results here meet or even exceed those of other areas of the world.

## Salience Of Joint Policy

In order to determine how relevant the Nordic collective manage-ment effort is to the needs and demands of the Nordic countries, we will discuss the salience of joint public policy. It is quite possible that the broad scope and fairly intensive policy-making process of the Nordic effort still is only concerned with nonessential issues of little relevance to the needs of the region. In particular, it would be valuable to deter-mine how issues of different salience have been handled on a Nordic basis. Are the more salient policy areas less often handled through joint processes and, if so, are these efforts less intensive than for the nonessential issues? In order to address ourselves to this question, we need some criteria for the determination of which issues are more salient than others.

Several analysts have discussed various ways to operationalize the concept of salience of policy.[14] It has been pointed out that there are severe difficulties with finding a generally agreed on rank ordering of various issue-areas. Not only does the importance of policy areas differ between societies and value systems, but also over time as the needs and goals of society change. Stanley Hoffmann has made a classic distinction between "high" and "low" politics, which he feels could serve as a universal dichotomy between salient and nonsalient issues.[15] This typology has been widely discussed in the literature on integration, as Hoffmann has argued that success-ful regional integration is merely confined to "low" politics. According

## NORDIC HANDLING OF "HIGH" AND "LOW" POLITICS AREAS

| "High" Politics | Dominant Type Neg. | Pos. |
|---|---|---|
| Military Security | X | |
| Diplomatic Influence | | X |
| Political Participation | X | |
| Public Safety and Order | | X |
| Economic and Military Aide | | X |
| Legal-Normative System | | X |

| "Low" Politics | Dominant Type Neg. | Pos. |
|---|---|---|
| Commercial Relations with other polities | X | |
| Economic development and promotion | | X |
| Regulation of business, labor and agriculture | X | |
| Control of economic system, monetary and fiscal policy | X | |
| Culture and recreation | | X |
| Social welfare | | X |
| Education and research | | X |

The Table is adapted from a similar table in Leon Lindberg and Stuart Scheingold, Europe's Would Be Polity (Englewood Cliffs: Prentice-Hall, 1971), p. 263, Figure 8:1.

to him, "high" politics is fairly immune to integration schemes since these issues involve questions of national identity, sovereignty, and power. In addition, Leon Lindberg and Stuart Scheingold have shown that the role of the European Community is extremely limited in "high" politics areas. [16] It is of interest to see how the Nordic group has handled issues of "high" and "low" politics.

In Table 4:4 we have divided the various policy areas listed in Table 4:3 between "high" and "low" politics. [17] We see that there are no significant differences in the scope or intensity of joint policy between the two types of issues. The Nordic countries seem to have processed "high" politics issues jointly to the same degree as they have achieved joint policy in "low" politics area. Thus, if one claims that "high" politics issues are more salient and less easily coordinated, we can observe that the Nordic policy output covers many of these salient issues.

There are several critics of the "high-low" politics concept. One has argued that this dichotomy is better seen as a continuum on a scale of policy salience, that what is "high" politics in one region or time period might be regarded as "low" politics in another setting and that today economic welfare issues are often handled as "high" politics.[18] In line with this critique, we will evaluate the salience of joint Nordic policy on a continuum of societal relevance. While it is rather fruitless to try to construct a generally acceptable rank ordering of numerous policy areas, one can claim that some broadly defined societal functions are more crucial than others.

We argue that the function of protecting the physical security of the people in society is the most important concern of the public authorities. Secondly, the question of material survival comes to mind. Thirdly, there is a need to maintain social order and stability. Fourthly, various welfare issues need to be satisfied. Finally, there are several other needs that must be handled, such as individual fulfillment, social status, prestige, and meaningful leisure activity. We can now look at how well the joint Nordic effort has handled these different societal functions. It is our expectation that the more crucial the function the less it has been handled in a joint manner and resulted in joint Nordic policy.

We observed in the preceding section that there is a formal split on security policy in the Nordic region. In this area, only very informal,

TABLE 4:5

## RANK ORDERING OF ISSUE-AREAS

1. Security Policy
2. Economic issues
3. Political participation, public order and health
4. Welfare, education
5. Culture, recreation

and less intensive, forms of joint policy coordination were found.
The area of economic policy has a mixed record. On the one hand
many issue-areas were found to have a very low intensity of joint
policy-making. On the other hand, some considerable joint policy
results have been achieved in a few economic areas, such as economic
development, exploitation of natural resources, and transportation.
Whenever questions of joint control or supervision of national economic
policy are involved, the results are few. In contrast, in areas where
problems associated with the small size of the national economies
can be overcome through larger joint efforts the achievements have
been considerable. Thus, while the separate national economic systems
are kept intact, each country can benefit from joint investments, exploitation, planning, and international representation. In the area
of social order and stability considerable efforts toward joint policy
are made. For example, legal systems, the maintenance of order,
public health, and access to political participation are often coordinated. Similarly, social welfare, education, culture, and recreation
are all subject to intensive joint policy-making.

We find that the Nordic countries have been most successful in
joint management of less salient issues. However, the maintenance
of social order and some questions concerning continued material
well being are also processed in a joint manner. We can also mention
that the salience has increased somewhat during the last ten years.
In particular, advances in intensity have been made in economic
issues since the early 1960s. These issues have increasingly come
to be included in the joint effort and thus have expanded Nordic
public policy into more salient areas. We also previously noted that
many areas of "high" politics are included in these joint efforts of

100

policy coordination. We can conclude this section by pointing to the relatively high salience of many aspects of joint Nordic policy. The output of these processes is by no means limited to nonessential types of public policy.

* * * * * * * * * * * * *

If we were to evaluate the results of the Nordic management process in terms of the output of joint policy, we can say that the scheme has been very successful in most issue-areas. Notable exceptions are security-defense and economic questions, where the negative type of policy coordination still prevails. Although this procedure might be less favorable to the region as a whole than a positive coordination system would be, there is a case for its advantages over positive coordination to the national units in the region. For various domestic and external reasons, some of the governments prefer the more informal, less controversial solution of negative coordination over the more noticeable and dramatic positive type in these more salient policy areas. So, it might be good national policy to keep the joint effort at a low intensity level in security and economic spheres.

101

# 5. The Nordic Way

The increasing role of transnational actors and linkages is of interest to analysts of contemporary international relations. We have argued here that the political authorities often see a need to collectively manage these forces in order to maintain the effective control of their societies. In this study we have seen how the North European effort of policy coordination was brought about by a desire to control as well as benefit from the various regional ties at the societal level. Increasing societal interconnections have made for trans-governmental interactions, institutional growth, and joint Nordic policy.

## Major Findings

We have found that the Nordic societies are knit together in fairly intensive networks of regional transactions in multiple areas. In addition, the Nordic flows are significantly more intensive than transfers with the external regions. The exchange of messages across the national boundaries within the Nordic region is particularly substantial. However, during the last ten years, a clear trend of increased external penetration of the Nordic societies is evident in this type of transaction. Thus, the overwhelming dominance of Nordic communications during the 1950s is today somewhat eroded, due to increased external exposures. Yet, the Nordic flows of mail and telephone calls still far outweigh any external exchanges.

The regional trade pattern shows an opposite trend from the flows of messages. While traditionally, Nordic trade has had a very limited place in the total foreign trade of each of the Nordic countries, these regional transactions are today of significant proportions. During the 1960s an impressive expansion of Nordic trade can be noted, while at the same time the Nordic societies have become relatively less closely tied to other regions in Europe.

The regional transfers of people are fairly stable throughout our twenty-year period. However, the exchanges of people within the Nordic region clearly outweighs the flows from and to any other region. This characterization is valid both for the general migration flows and for the transfers of foreign students. We also noted that Nordic migration results in permanent changes of residence and citizenship to a greater extent than do the external flows.

The general impression of the Nordic transaction flows during 1952-1972 is that of high regional rates combined with marked discontinuities between the region and the external areas. For all types except trade, the Nordic flows were already very intensive in 1952 and significantly more intensive than the external exchanges. Except for a marked increase in regional trade during the 1960s, the Nordic societies have not experienced any drastic increase in mutual relevance during the period studied. Instead, high rates of mutual transfers have characterized the region of a considerable time. While the volumes of Nordic flows have grown, the proportion of regional transactions to total foreign exchanges has not increased substantially. It has sometimes even declined. The region was already in 1952 closely tied together by various flows and the changes from that time to now have not been significant, except for the trade data.

The trans-Nordic activities of various elite groups provided another dimension of transnational community to be explored. Traditionally, these transnational activities have been channeled through informal and flexible means, such as private contacts, letters, and telephone calls. Central institutions, such as permanent secretariats, have only very recently been established. This recent reorganization of the structure of trans-Nordic interactions has been coupled with an intensification of the interactions themselves. It now seems that the ambitions of these regional activities are not only to exchange information, develop joint positions, and take part in joint projects, but also to try to influence the newly established joint public institutions in the area. However, this new goal is still secondary to the more traditional functions of working jointly in favor of certain interests and ideas through the separate national administrations.

The growth of transnational elite activities in the Nordic region has experienced a two-step development. First, contacts were initiated in an effort to manage common problems resulting from the high mutual relevance of the Nordic societies. The regional activities were at this time mainly responses to developments at the aggregate level of societal relations and cannot be characterized as aiming at influencing the joint governmental decision-making process. Later, the trans-Nordic contacts were channeled into more structured, formal, and institutional means. An effort was made to create joint coordinating bodies that could ensure continuous exposure to regional considerations and serve as spokesmen for the national organizations in their dealings with the joint governmental institutions in the region. At this time, the transnational interactions intensified as contacts with the joint public organs became more important. The goal of influencing the joint governmental policy-making process also became one of the major ambitions of the trans-Nordic activities. As before, many aspects of these interest group oriented activities are targeted at the national administrations but a second focus towards the joint institutions has also developed.

We have also seen that the various groups coordinate their domestic activities on an extensive scale. Thus, while their participation in the joint public policy-making process is yet of more limited importance, the coordination of nationally oriented activity and positions is crucial. Continuous contacts are maintained on a trans-Nordic basis to develop similar strategies, policy positions, and attitudes on major domestic issues. Here the goal is not to approach the governments jointly but to reach joint positions that can be presented to the various national governments. Thus, the transnational relations can have considerable impact on the positions taken on a wide range of issues within each Nordic society. In this regard, the role of transnational activities and linkages is crucial for an understanding of the relations within as well as among advanced industrial societies.

— — — — — — — — — — — —

In line with most forms of international cooperation, the joint institutions operating in the Nordic region are not in any sense supranational. These bodies cannot be seen as decision-making centers that are independent of the separate national governments in the area. Instead, the joint structures serve to facilitate the collective policy-making process among the governments in the region.[1] This is done by ensuring that regional perspectives are maintained in the deliberations, by aiding interactions and communications among the national officials involved, and by keeping the joint process flowing continuously and steadily.

We have seen how the secretariats of the Nordic Council and Council of Ministers have brought important initiatory and mediative functions to the joint enterprise.[2] By carrying out these functions, the joint institutions give valuable promotive effects to the cooperation effort. However, we also noted that the cooperation process was very intensive and resulted in substantial policy outputs before the establishment of such permanent, joint institutions. Thus, the promotive effects of such international organs are not always necessary for accomplishing joint ventures. Rather, they mainly help give some stability, continuity, and possibly speed to the collective coordination effort.[3]

Probably, there is less need for such permanency and formalization of the interactions among the countries in the Nordic region than in most other areas. In most international cooperation efforts, joint organs would be very important to give structural rigor and a sense of permanence and seriousness to the joint efforts. In the Nordic region, the tradition of joint consultations and the close ties among the political and bureaucratic participants require less of the kind of formalization and structural rigor that keeps other international efforts flowing.

The officials working in the various joint Nordic secretariats are mainly concerned with promoting Nordic cooperation. In contrast to the numerous national officials participating in the joint policy-making process, these Nordic officials maintain a clear regional perspective on issues and help facilitiate suitable compromise solutions. For this reason, one can easily conclude that the international officials stand in some kind of opposition to the national officials, who generally try to protect specific national interests. However, we have found that one important resource available to the Nordic officials is their ability to reach into the national administrations for support on regional issues.

Thus, it seems more important for international officials to be able to cooperate smoothly with their national counterparts than to try to gain as much independence as possible from national authority. National governments generally maintain effective control of the most crucial aspects of international cooperation. So, if the international officials want to stay inside the joint policy-making process and not be assigned primarily administrative or implementive functions, they need to keep in close contact with their national colleagues.[4]

The international officials have ample opportunity to promote joint ventures and solutions by discrete and low-key undertakings. In this effort, the roles of initiator, mediator, and sometimes vetoer, can easily fall on the international officials. In particular, the role of initiator of new regional policy is important. In the Nordic area, the joint Nordic officials are the main initiators of proposals or ideas for new joint ventures. This is done by the parliamentary officials of the Nordic Council, who initiate proposals for recommendations by that body, and by the Nordic ministerial officials who generally set the agendas for the ministerial deliberations. The important point is that the international officials take the initiative and make the national participants mainly respondents to ideas or proposals forwarded from a joint Nordic perspective. Although the crucial level of decision lies with the national administrations, particularly the high-level officials assisting the ministers, the international officials can have considerable impact on the policy results through their initiative.

Similarly, the mediatory role of the Nordic officials proved to be an important means to enhance joint solutions that also benefit the regional actors. Often, the joint deliberations are based on suggestions for compromise solutions presented by the Nordic officials. Thus, these officials can set the guidelines for the joint effort through their mediatory role.

The international actors build coalitions with other actors in the region to help increase their impact on the joint policy-making process. Often, the joint secretariats can get support from some of the national administrations in an effort for new cooperative schemes. For example, the Finnish representative in the Council of Ministers has generally supported the budget proposals by the joint secretariats. Similarly, the support of corresponding governmental agencies in several countries help increase the possibilities for general acceptance of a proposal. This way, the national governments are affected by the pressure from both the international secretariat itself and from some part of their own administration. The support of the various administrations is often acquired by having the national officials participate in the early stages of policy formulation and investigation. That way, each national representative can identify with the final product of these deliberations and, presumably, work for its acceptance by the government.

107

Often the strongest resistance to new joint policy is found in the national bureaucracies.[5] The Nordic officials then need to enlist the support of the political leaders of the region. In the Council of Ministers system of policy-making it is very difficult to get around strong opposition at the bureaucratic level. The national officials, meeting in various Permanent Committees of High Officials, are effective vetoers of new policy as they determine the items that will be discussed by the ministers and the issues with which the secretariats should be involved. However, the Nordic officials have some possibilities to reach the political leaders directly. This can be done by enlisting the support of the parliamentary sphere of cooperation. In fact, intensive collaboration between the ministerial and parliamentary officials could result in a more effective regional impact on the decentralized policy-making process in the area. The parliamentary officials are generally open to suggestions for new policy proposals even in the face of strong national bureaucratic resistence. This way, the national ministers are also made aware of the ideas and, if they find them attractive, argue in their favor against the national officials. Strong parliamentary support in the Nordic Council for the proposal can then be used as leverage on the national bureaucracies.[6]

As we noted above, that a close and mutually responsive relationship between the national and international officials is important for the latters' ability to influence decision-making, it is crucial that strategies directed against the national bureaucracies are carried out very discreetly and only on a limited number of issues. If the Nordic actors are to gain the trust and support of the national officials, who generally are the most important actors in the joint process, they cannot openly and dramatically work against the interests of these officials. Instead, low-key informal efforts must be made to put political pressure on the national bureaucracies.

— — — — — — — — — — — —

The most important aspect of joint policy-making in the Nordic region is the extensive and intensive interactions among various governmental elites across national boundaries. One important characteristic of the trans-Nordic networks is that they exist across the national administrations and are not channeled through any single forum. Thus, this bureaucratic interpenetration is both broad in scope and reaches

108

deep inside the separate national administrations. One could say that the 'zone of contact' [7] among the Nordic governmental bureaucracies is very large.

In particular, the informal means of trans-Nordic contacts should be emphasized here. Outside of periodic formal meetings, the national officials responsible for policy planning, formulation, and implementation engage in continuous exchanges of letters and telephone calls with their counterparts in the neighboring countries. Due to this constant exposure to regional perspectives, national policy is often formulated jointly by the Nordic governments. In a previous chapter we discussed the considerable policy coordination that has been achieved in the region largely through this process of decentralized policy-making. [8]

We have also found that the frequency of bureaucratic interactions, at least in formal meetings, seems to vary with the political interests and directions of the time. Thus, the role of political leadership would seem to be an important stimulating factor in this process and make for substantially meaningful interactions. This observation leads us to the conclusion that policy coordination is dependent on political decisions and moods and does not result from bureaucratic interpenetration alone. Although the national officials can acquire greater exposure and larger perspectives through continuous trans-national contacts, political leadership is necessary to give the bureaucratic interactions direction and meaning. [9]

We noted that the interactions among the national officials were not channeled through any central, coordinating body but were taking place throughout the national administrations and at all levels. Thus, the governmental control and direction of these bureaucratic contacts can be far less than effective. It is interesting to inquire into the consequences of these transgovernmental relations on national policy formulation and coherence.

Traditionally, Nordic issues have been treated more as an extension of domestic policy-making than as relations with foreign powers. [10] Thus, the need for nationally coherent and centralized positions have seemed less pressing than the ability for each governmental agency independently to coordinate its activities with its regional counterparts. In fact, to many officials central governmental coordination and direction would be seen as an unnecessary and obstructive interference in their 'practical and non-political' activities. No doubt, these uncoordinated and multiple transactions across the national administrations in the region cannot be treated as expressions of a country's foreign policy in a traditional sense. Instead, the term trans-governmental relations would be more suitable for these interactions. On Nordic issues it is also fairly meaningless to distinguish between domestic and foreign policy in the region, as these issues are handled primarily outside of the national foreign ministries. [11]

During the last years, the Nordic governments have become aware of this process of trans-governmental relations and have tried to increase central control. [12] One of the main features of the recent institution-alization of the collective policy-making process is the greater national coordination and control possible under the new structures. For example, the Committee of Deputies is charged with general coordination of the separate cooperation efforts within each functional committee. The national representatives in this body are also assisted by staffs that try to work out nationally coherent policies. It is typical that the foreign ministries in the region provide the staff for this effort of national coordination.

Thus, during the last five years some restraints have been placed on the previously very loosely organized trans-governmental relations.[13] However, central control is still far less concerning Nordic issues than in other areas. For example, each of the fourteen Permanent Committees of High Officials is responsible for its functional area of cooperation and its members report directly to their own ministers.[14]

In the long run, the crucial role of the Committee of Deputies in the joint budget process could have considerable centralizing effects on the activities in the separate cooperation areas. It is not surprising that this body presently is trying to include all sectors of the Nordic cooperation effort into one large joint budget. It is particularly interesting that the large cultural sector so far has maintained its own joint budget, determined by the ministers of culture themselves. Thus, central control of this area of cooperation would seem to be rather limited and primarily dependent on the ability to influence each national ministry separately.

One of the most important questions arising from international cooperation and policy-making is the possibility for democratic control of and participation in these processes.[15] In the Nordic region the

110

Nordic Council represents the parliamentary side of this cooperation effort.  Due to the very uncoordinated, low-key, and informal means used for Nordic ministerial cooperation, the hopes for effective parliamentary control of these activities are rather small.  The national parliaments find it extremely difficult to control the direction of the trans-governmental relations and can generally not invalidate solutions already agreed upon in joint deliberations.  To improve the chances for domestic control of this bureaucratic inter-penetration, affecting a large number of important political issues, some efforts have been made to use the Nordic Council as a device for parliamentary supervision.

One of the main targets of this parliamentary control has been the joint Nordic budgets.  It is hoped that parliamentary participation in the budget process will increase the democratic responsiveness of the mainly bureaucratic activities in the area.  So far, the impact of the Nordic Council has been very limited.  The reasons for this result are found in an inability to make substantive contributions on the part of the parliamentarians and in a lack of cooperation and openness on the ministerial side.  For example, often the budget is, in reality, finalized before the parliamentary views are heard and these political leaders are generally denied access to internal governmental materials, such as minutes, memos, requests for funds, etc. Thus, the democratic control of the joint ministerial budget making process is marginal and in no way corresponds to the parliamentary impact on the national scene.

As an increasingly large part of national policy is developed through these joint activities it seems questionable from the stand-point of democratic values that the parliamentary input is so limited.  Possibly, the parliamentary activities could be increased in the national legislatures.  This way each national administration would be made responsible for its actions in these trans-governmental interactions.  Transnational party strategies to simultaneously bring up some Nordic issue in all five parliaments could prove valuable and increase parliamentary participation in the region.  Political awareness of and participation in Nordic cooperation will most likely not increase until these issues are brought into the domestic political debates in each of the five countries.  The role of transnational party groupings could here be very important to bring a new democratic dimension to the joint policy-making process.

— — — — — — — — — — — —

When reviewing the policy results of the collective management effort, we noted the broad scope and varying intensity of Nordic policy. While questions concerning the stimulation of transnational flows and the sharing of scarce resources have been successfully handled, issues related to protection from external disturbances are less far reaching. Here, the basic national orientation of each government seems to have limited the extent to which the political elites are willing to accept restraints. The dilemma between policy effectiveness and governmental autonomy has been settled in favor of maximum autonomy and minimum effectiveness. However, we must also underscore that the Nordic management effort has produced numerous joint policies of significance to the region. In comparison with other experiments in coping, the Nordic results are probably greater in quantity although they might restrict national objectives and strategies as much as some.

The Nordic technique might be best suited to the needs of governments with strong commitments to societal engineering and change. Here the pursuit of domestic objectives is given priority over regional considerations placing restraints on the attainment of those goals. The political elites can participate in the Nordic management process without fear of undermining their authority or compromising their values and ideals. Only when national objectives can be achieved through collective policy will the political elites commit themselves to a joint solution. [16]

## Major Lessons

What can be learned from the North European example of interest to analysts of other cases of coping with transnationalism? Most fundamentally, we have noted the basic national orientation of the participating actors in the management process. Even in the very homogenous, cohesive setting of Northern Europe the distinct domestic objectives and aspirations of the political elites often severly weaken efforts at regional solutions. If this is the case here, one would assume that other areas experiencing greater diversity and internal conflict will manifest even less willingness to set aside national priorities for the collective good. So, international collaboration processes can be best understood within the context of domestic politics and can not be viewed as existing above this arena. [17]

We have also seen how the governmental bureaucracies remain the most crucial actors. These can both speed up the management process and, more commonly, slow it down. Often, the government officials responsible for the administration of a particular policy area find it convenient to oppose, resist, or obstruct collective efforts. If they feel their position of authority within the political elite might be threatened by joint policy they will strongly oppose any such move. Similarly, deviations from traditional policy will be resisted if the perceived risks of undertaking new action with uncertain effects or outcomes are major. [18]

In order to launch collective management strategies it is often necessary to overcome this bureaucratic inertia and fear of change. Here, commitment by the political leaders can be important. Pressure applied by the ministers, parliamentarians, or political parties to enlist their support. However, as the political leadership generally relies heavily on the permanent officials for information, counsel, and recommendations, more often than not the bureaucratic suspicions and hesitations are transmitted into the leadership stratum as well. [19] International secretariats seemed to play an important part in helping to overcome this tendency. Trans-governmental coalitions among national officials and politicians were promoted by the secretariats to build support for their proposals. Close direct contacts with the political leaders were also maintained to present an alternative view to that offered by the national officials. This way, the government officials' veto power over new policy initiatives was somewhat lessened to allow for the consideration of fresh ideas.

We observed how central political control of trans-governmental contacts has been increased in Northern Europe during recent years. The trend has not only been toward more intense, functionally oriented interactions making up a cobweb of ties and commitments. At the same time, an effort has emerged to centralize and oversee these disperse relations. Thus, the functionalist challenge has been met by traditional inter-governmental management techniques to try to maintain effective authority over external relations. Overall, North European interactions are less stringently controlled than other foreign relations. Yet, one sees an attempt at asserting Foreign Ministry authority even in this case of regional harmony and stability, where such control would appear to be less urgent than elsewhere. [20]

113

The motive behind collective management is a desire to protect the societies and regimes from drastic change. Transnational forces constantly threaten to disrupt existing structures and make for undirected change leading to unknown outcomes. To avoid this uncertainty and potentially unstable situation, the political elites find it useful to engage in collective management. This process is aimed more at conserving the familiar, acceptable existence of the present than to promote new relationships for the future.[21] The political elites are not building a future but simply repairing an existence, which is constantly under attack from social and economic developments. For this reason, no explicit goals or aspirations for the collective work are evident. As the process involves more patch-work than construction, there is no clear target to work toward and no uniform image of what the future will bring. The ambition is simply to cope and not be overcome by events.

* * * * * * * * * * * * * * * *

Throughout this study we have discussed how the five Nordic countries have tried to solve national problems and issues through joint processes. This regional cooperation effort is firmly based on the principle of formal national sovereignty and independence. Although there is a firm commitment to joint cooperation and a realization of the mutual benefits possible from larger solutions than the national ones, the political leaders of the region have no explicit ambitions or hopes of creating a future Nordic super-state. Instead, the cooperation process is characterized by mutual restraints and willingness to compromise, combined with respect for the autonomy of each of the participants. Often, the countries manage to reach joint solutions but at other times the result is harmonious diversity.

The crucial point about these efforts toward mutually satisfying solutions is not so much the periodic failures or dramatic successes, but the existence of a continuous, uninterrupted process of consultation, deliberation, and decision. This process might seem slow and unexciting when compared to other more dramatic and politicized cooperation efforts. However, the strength of the Nordic management process is its perseverance and commitment to continued cooperation even at times of great failures or serious external challenges.

For believers in quick solutions to the problems facing the world, the Nordic approach is no answer. The Nordic strategy of coping with transnationalism is stable, but slow and incremental. There are very few great achievements, but also few sudden disappointments. This strategy of international cooperation might not be as fascinating as some others practiced, but perhaps it is more relevant to our world of increasing interdependencies in need of joint political solutions.

# Notes

## Chapter 1
## The Challenge of Transnationalism

1. For a discussion of transnational relations see; Robert Keohane and Joseph Nye, eds., Transnational Relations and World Politics (Cambridge: Harvard University Press, 1971) and Werner Feld, Nongovernmental Forces and World Politics (New York: Praeger, 1972).

2. Interdependence has been discussed among others by; Oran Young, "Interdependencies in World Politics," International Journal, Vol. 24 (1969), 726-750, Edward Morse, Modernization and the Transformation of International Relations (New York: Free Press,1976), Robert Keohane and Joseph Nye, Power and Interdependence (Boston: Little, Brown, 1977).

3. Robert Keohane and Joseph Nye, "Power and Interdependence," Survival, Vol. 15, No. 4 (July/August 1973), 158-165.

4. Gerhard Mally, Interdependence (Lexington: Lexington Books, 1976), Robert Keohane and Joseph Nye, "International Interdependence and Integration," in Fred Greenstein and Nelson Polsby, eds., The Handbook of Political Science, Vol. 8, (Reading, Mass.:. Addision-Wesley, 1975), pp. 363-414, and special issues of International Organization, Vol. 29, No. 1 and No.3 on "World Politics and International Economics" and "International Responses to Technology".

5. Robert Keohane and Joseph Nye, "Trans-governmental Relations and International Organization," World Politics, Vol. 27, No. 1 (October 1974), 39-62, Karl Kaiser, "Transnational Politics: Toward a Theory of Multinational Politics," International Organization, Vol. 25, No. 4 (Autumn 1971), 790-817, Lawrence Scheinman, "Economic Regionalism

and International Administration: The European Communities Experience," in Robert S. Jordan, ed., International Administration (New York: Oxford University Press, 1971), pp. 187-227.

6. Gerhard Mally, op. cit., Robert Keohane and Joseph Nye, op. cit., Annette Baker Fox, The Politics of Attraction (New York: Columbia University Press, 1976), and the special issue of International Organization, Vol. 28, No. 4 (Autumn 1974) on "Canada and the United States: Transnational and Transgovernmental Relations".

7. Lawrence Scheinman, op. cit., Donald Puchala, "Of Blind Men, Elephants, and International Integration," Journal of Common Market Studies, Vol. 10, No. 3 (March 1972), 267-284, Idem., "Domestic Politics and Regional Harmonization in the European Communities", World Politics, Vol. 27, No. 4 (July 1975), 496-520, Ernst Haas, The Obsolescence of Regional Integration Theory (Berkely: Institute of International Studies, 1975), Helen Wallace, et. al., eds., Policy-Making in the European Community (New York: John Wiley, 1977).

8. Amitai Etzioni, "A Stable Union: The Nordic Associational Web 1953-1964," in Political Unification (New York: Holt, Rinehart, Winston, 1965), pp. 184-228.

9. Nils Andren, "Nordic Integration: Aspects and Problems," Cooperation and Conflict, Vol. 2, No. 1 (1967), 1-25.

10. A Critique of the Andren essay is provided in; Barbara Haskel, "Is There an Unseen Spider?" Cooperation and Conflict, Vol. 2 No. 3-4 (1967), 229-234.

11. Stanley Anderson, The Nordic Council (Seattle: University of Washington Press, 1967). A review is found in: Barbara Haskel, "Regionalism without Politics," Cooperation and Conflict, Vol. 3, No. 3 (1968), 195-198.

12. Nils Orvik, "Nordic Cooperation and High Politics," International Organization, Vol. 28, No. 1 (Winter 1974), 61-88.

13. See for example, Nils Orvik, "Integration-For Whom, Against Whom?" Cooperation and Conflict, Vol. 2, No. 1 (1967), 54-59.

14. Barbara Haskel, The Scandinavian Option (Oslo: Universitetsforlaget, 1976).

15. Erik Solem, The Nordic Council and Scandinavian Integration, (New York: Praeger, 1977).

16. Robert Dickerman, "Transgovernmental Challenge and Response in Scandinavia and North America," International Organization, Vol. 30, No. 2 (Spring 1976), 213-240.

17. Bengt Sundelius, "Transgovernmental Interactions in the Nordic Region," Cooperation and Conflict, Vol. 12, No. 2 (1977), 63-86.

18. An excellent bibliography is found in Bernt Schiller, Books, Articles, Reports Concerning Nordic Cooperation, Nordisk Utredningsserie 1975:3, (Stockholm: Nordic Council, 1975).

# Chapter 2
## A Transnational Community

1. Nordic Council, Annual Record, 1969, Supplement, p. 24.

2. Statistics provided by Mr. Sten Lindgren, Swedish Federation of Industry.

3. Nordic Council, Annual Record, 1969, Supplement, p. 25.

# Chapter 3
## The Collective Management Process

1. Quoted in Barbara Haskel, The Scandinavian Option (Oslo: Universitetsforlaget, 1976), p. 162.

2. Nordic Council, Nordiska Samarbetsorgan, (Stockholm: 1974).

3. This assumption does not hold completely as we know that intra-cabinet rivalry and struggle for increased funds take place on this level as well and can show up in the regional dealings.

4. Nordic Council, Kalendarium, 1964, 1974, (Stockholm: 1964, 1974).

5. Emile Noel and Henri Etienne, "The Permanent Representatives Committee and the Deepening of the Communities," in Ghita Ionescu, ed., The New Politics of European Integration, (London: Macmillan, 1972), p. 123.

6. Roy Pryce, The Politics of the European Community (Totowa, New Jersey: Rowman & Littlefield, 1973), p. 79.

7. When one sees this figure for the EC meetings, one is struck by the great demand on the national administration that these frequent meetings involve. For example, Denmark, which participates both in the EC meetings and the Nordic interactions, must be faced with severe

pressures to be able to actively participate in and have an impact on the numerous meetings. Observers have also noted that Denmark has had some difficulty giving sufficient attention to the Nordic issues since its entry into the Common Market.

8. This data are based on a mail-questionnaire sent to over two hundred of the leading parliamentarians, national officials, and Nordic officials involved in Nordic interactions. The response rate was 61%, which made for a final sample of 126 individuals, all identified as active participants in regional affairs.

9. The great language similarities have most likely contributed to this practice.

10. Somewhat of a curiosity is the fact that as early as in 1818 a Swedish Royal decree instructed all Swedish agencies and officials to communicate directly with their counterparts in Norway to make their interactions smoother and more efficient. At that time, Sweden and Norway were united in a union under the same Head of State, the Swedish monarch. However, this union had two separate governments, national administrations, and political systems and only the foreign relations were handled jointly. In an administrative sense they were two separate entities. See, Hans Blix, Statsmyndingheternas Internationella Forbindelser (Stockholm: Nordstedts, 1964), p. 215.

11. This information was given by the Director of the switchboard. Naturally, this figure is very approximate and only used to illustrate the great disparity between Nordic telephone exchanges and other external communications.

12. Thomas Anton, "Policy-Making and Political Culture in Sweden", Scandinavian Political Studies, Vol. 4 (Oslo: Universitetsforlaget, 1969), 99.

13. Ibid., p. 94.

14. For example, see; Amitai Etzioni, Political Unification (New York: Holt, Rinehart, Winston, 1965),p. 323.

15. These negotiations are analyzed by Barbara Haskel in op. cit. Chapter 3.

16. Ernst Haas, "International Integration; The European and the Universal Process," International Organization, Vol. 15, No. 3 (Summer 1961), 367-368.

17. We will here adopt the role categories suggested in Robert Cox and Harold Jacobson, eds., The Anatomy of Influence (New Haven: Yale University Press, 1973),p. 12.

18. The information presented in this section is mainly based on open-ended interviews with approximately fifty participants in this process of interaction, as well as on participant-observation by the writer. Due to the necessity of discretion and respect for the anonymity of the individuals interviewed, personal references will not be given.

One basic limitation with the analysis offered here is the neglect to specify the particular issue-area treated. Rather, the study tries to present the module pattern of Nordic interactions. Naturallly, deviations from this basic model can be found in particular issue-areas. An interesting task for a later study would be to determine where and why such deviations occur.

19. It is worth noting that before 1972 these officials were the only ones working full time with Nordic cooperation. Suddenly, a competing structure appeared which could easily gain dominance in the cooperation process.

20. This figure excludes the statements made by the committee chairmen, who by virtue of their position participate lively in the meetings. The four parliamentary chairmen made a total of 109 statements in the meetings.

21. The data is based on participant observation during September-October 1974.

22. Here, the important issue of democratic control and leadership over the bureaucracy must be raised. If the officials of the Council act as the vetoers of the decision-making process, while the parliamentarians serve as the controllers we find our common notions of political decision-making somewhat confused. The reason for this situation is not to be found in any usurpation of power on the part of the staff, but is simply a result of a lack of activity, interest, and sufficient time for Nordic questions on the part of most parliamentarians. This attitude is understandable, as the nationally elected politicians must primarily serve their national constituencies in their parliaments. However, the low degree of involvement in and concern for Nordic cooperation issues by most parliamentarians is noteworthy as it distorts the parliamentary-political functions of the Council.

23. Robert Russell makes a similar observation regarding international monetary relations: "Transgovernmental coalitions - seem to rise and fall in impact with the salience and controversiality of the issue.

121

- As policy decisions were elevated to the level of heads of government and became publicly debated in legislatures, the resources which transgovernmental coalitions could mobilize to influence policy decisions became less and less decisive for the outcomes." Robert Russell, "Transgovernmental Interaction in the International Monetary System 1960-1972," International Organization, Vol. 27, No. 4 (Autumn 1973), 464.

24. Nordic Council, Riktlinjer for Nordiskt Kultursamarbete, Nordisk Utredningsserie 24/74, (Stockholm: 1974), p. 5.

25. Lawrence Scheinman notes the generally protective attitudes of national administrators in the EC as well. According to Scheinman, the fundamental concern with system maintenance combined with an interest in European cooperation put these national officials in a serious dilemma. Lawrence Scheinman, "Some Preliminary Notes on Bureaucratic Relationships in the EEC," International Organization, Vol. 20, No. 4 (Autumn 1966), 763.

26. Robert Cox and Harold Jacobson, eds., op. cit., p. 428.

## Chapter 4
## Achievements and Failures

1. A comprehensive, although dated, overview of the Nordic accomplishments is The Nordic Council and Cooperation in Scandinavia (Copenhagen: Munksgaard, 1959) by the long-time Danish Secretary General of the Nordic Council, Frantz Wendt. Also see Erik Solem, The Nordic Council and Scandinavian Integration (New York: Praeger, 1977) and Nordisk Rad i 25 Ar (Stockholm: Foreningen Nordens Forbund, 1977) published for the silver anniversary of the Council.

2. Leon Lindberg and Stuart Scheingold, Europe's Would Be Polity (Englewood Cliffs: Prentice-Hall, 1970), p. 60.

3. For an analysis of Nordic security policies, see Johan Jorgen Holst, ed., Five Roads to Nordic Security (Oslo: Universitetsforlaget, 1973).

4. Phillipe Schmitter, "A Revised Theory of Regional Integration," International Organization, Vol. 24, No. 4 (Autumn 1970), 836-868.

5. Ernst Haas and Edward T. Rowe, "Regional Organizations in the United Nations: Is There Externalization?" International Studies Quarterly, Vol. 17, No. 1 (March 1973), 3-54.

6. Kurt Jacobsen, "Voting Behavior of the Nordic Countries in the General Assembly," Jaako Kalela, "The Nordic Group in the General Assembly," Jan-Erik Lidstrom and Claes Wiklund, "The Nordic Countries in the General Assembly and Its Two Political Committees," all in Cooperation and Conflict, Vol. 2, No. 3-4 (1967), 139-187.

7. For a review of the joint Nordic efforts in the area of development assistance, see the publication by the five Nordic development agencies on the subject. Swedish International Development Authority, Nordiskt Samarbete for U-Landerna (Stockholm: SIDA, 1974).

8. The bridge-building concept is critically discussed in Niels Amstrup and Carsten Sorensen, "Denmark: Bridge between the Nordic Countries and the European Community?", Cooperation and Conflict, Vol. 10, No. 1-2 (1975), 21-32.

9. Nordic Council, Annual Record, 1975, C1, p. 52.

10. An excellent study of these activities in English is Ingeborg Lyche, Nordic Cultural Cooperation (Oslo: Universitetsforlaget, 1974).

11. Nordic Council, Nordiskt Samarbete inom forskningens och den hogre undervisningens omrade, Nordisk Udredningsserie 1967/2, (Stockholm: Nordic Council, 1967).

12. This effort is analyzed in Barbara Haskel, The Scandinavian Option (Oslo: Universitetsforlaget, 1976).

13. This proposal is analyzed in Claes Wiklund, "The Zig-Zag Course of the Nordek Negotiations," Scandinavian Political Studies, Vol. 5 (Oslo: Universitetsforlaget, 1970), pp. 307-336.

14. Leon Lindberg, "Regional Integration as a Multidimensional Phenomenon Requiring Multivariable Measurements," In Leon Lindberg and Stuart Scheingold, eds., Regional Integration (Cambridge: Harvard University Press, 1971), p. 63.

15. Stanley Hoffman, "Discord in Community: The North Atlantic Area as a Partial International System," in Francis Wilcox and Field Haviland, eds., The Atlantic Community (New York: Praeger, 1963), pp. 3-31.

16. Leon Lindberg and Stuart Scheingold, op. cit., p. 263.

17. The selection of issue-areas into each category was made by Leon Lindberg and Stuart Scheingold in Ibid., p. 263.

18. For examples of this viewpoint see selections in the special issue on "Regional Integration: Theory and Research," of International Organization, Vol. 24, No. 4 (Autumn 1970).

## Chapter 5
## The Nordic Way

1. In the words of Keohane and Nye, we can most appropriately think of the Nordic organizations as "clusters of intergovernmental and transgovernmental networks associated with the formal institutions." Power and Interdependence (Boston: Little, Brown, 1977), p. 240.

2. The trend during the last ten years has been toward institution building as numerous small, new joint bodies have been created. Today, over one hundred permanent organizations and committees exist. See; Nordiska Samarbetsorgan (Stockholm: Nordic Council, 1977). This change is in contrast to the North American case. According to Holsti and Levy, no such trend can be found in U.S.-Canadian relations. Kal Holsti and Thomas Allen Levy, "Bilateral Institutions and Transgovernmental Relations Between Canada and the U.S.," International Organization, Vol. 28, No. 4 (Autumn 1974) 879, 880, 896.

3. Robert Keohane and Joseph Nye have found that in the U.S.-Canadian case the existence of solid transgovernmental networks proved a source of stability for the joint policy coordination effort. op. cit. p. 214. I would also argue that the foundation for Nordic activities is found in the transgovernmental interactions, but the actors participating in these are now better held accountable for their work by being forced to meet deadlines and produce results expected by outside groups.

4. Carole Webb has made a similar observation regarding the EC. She contends that "it is governments who decide the appropriate procedures for policy-making across the range of issues and not the issues themselves which objectively determine the process." "Introduction: Variations on a Theoretical Theme," in Helen Wallace, et. al., eds., Policy-Making in the European Community (New York: John Wiley, 1977), p. 22. Similarly, Robert W. Cox and Harold K. Jacobson, in their study of decision-making in international organizations, conclude that "viewing international organizations according to how far they involve the effective policy-making processes of governments rather than how independent of states they have become" might be a more useful way of approaching the subject. The Anatomy of Influence (New Haven: Yale University Press, 1974), p. 428.

5. This is also the case in the European Community. See Carole Webb in Ibid. p. 16.

6. It has been argued that also in the EC case the success of trans-governmental coalitions depends on the ability to bypass central coordinating bodies and to use the regional arena as a resource for settling intra-governmental conflicts. Ibid., p.23.

7. This concept was introduced by Gunnar Sjostedt, OECD-Samarbetet: Funktioner och Effekter, University of Stockholm Political Studies 3, (Stockholm: 1973), pp. 91-110.

8. Keohane and Nye have also found that the existence of "informal networks of working relationships at a lower level of the bureaucracy, among likeminded officials and those with similar tasks--will be crucial in effectively coordinating policy." op. cit., p. 233.

9. Lawrence Scheinman reaches a similar conclusion regarding the impact of bureaucratic interpenetration in the EC. He concludes that this process remains the foundation stone of European cooperation but that it alone is insufficient to push the joint policy-making effort forward. To this end, political decisions are necessary. "Some Preliminary Notes on Bureaucratic Relationships in the EEC," International Organization, Vol. 20, No. 4 (Autumn 1966), 773.

10. Robert Dickerman contends that the Scandinavian interactions have evolved from a situation of traditionally very tight central governmental control of administrative contacts to today's great tolerance of such contacts within the Nordic area. "Transgovernmental Challenge and Response in Scandinavia and North America," International Organization, Vol. 30, No. 2 (Spring 1976) 224. I would argue just the opposite. Nongovernmental and low level administrative contacts within functional areas have been carried out throughout the last century and in most instances these have been very loosely supervised by the foreign ministries. In fact, already in 1818 a Swedish Royal Decree instructed the national administrative agencies to deal directly with their counterparts in Norway. Also, in the 1962 Helsinki Agreement such direct administrative contacts were formally endorsed by the Nordic governments, who then merely codified a long established practice. See, Hans Blix, Statsmyndigheternas Internationella Forbindelser (Stockholm: Nordstedts, 1964).

11. Robert Dickerman asserts, on the basis of interviews with foreign ministry personnel, that the embassies in the Nordic capitals have an important role to play in overseeing the broad range of relations between the governments. Thus, the foreign ministries would retain

primary responsibility for regional affairs through the use of embassies as monitors of transgovernmental relations. op. cit., pp. 223,238. In my judgment, the capacity of these embassies to perform this function is totally indadequate and the assertion mainly reflects wishful thinking on the part of the diplomatic staffs, who find their impact on Nordic issues marginal.

12. This finding is contrary to Robert Dickerman's observation that the Scandinavians "denied using any particular internal control mechanism in dealing with this wide range of Nordic business--.." op. cit., p. 221.

13. These recent Nordic developments support Robert Keohane's and Joseph Nye's assertion that national policy-makers faced with the complexities of extensive trans-governmental relations will become increasingly concerned about losing national control over these activities. Keohane and Nye predict that demands for stricter national controls will be made to reassert national cohesion in policy. "Transgovernmental Relations and International Organization," World Politics, Vol. 27, No. 1 (October 1974) 61.

Also in the EC, observers have pointed to "an increase in governmental control as their political leaders seek to maintain a coordinating and directing role," Carole Webb, op. cit., pp. 19-20.

14. This also inhibits strategies of linking issues across functional areas. Each issue is negotiated on its own merits and linkages to other issue-areas are not generally regarded as appropriate or useful. Similar norms seem to dominate U.S.-Canadian relations. See Robert Keohane and Joseph Nye, Power and Interdependence (Boston: Little, Brown, 1977) pp. 171, 214, and Kal Holsti and Thomas Levy, op. cit., p. 884.

15. See the discussion of this aspect in Karl Kaiser, "Transnational Relations as a Threat to the Democratic Process," in Robert Keohane and Joseph Nye, eds., Transnational Relations and World Politics, (Cambridge: Harvard University Press. 1971), pp. 356-370.

16. A similar argument regarding the European Community is presented by Peter Busch and Donald Puchala in their "Interests, Influence, and Integration: Political Structure in the European Communities," Comparative Political Studies, Vol. 9, No. 3 (October 1976) 235-254.

17. Several analysts have come to similar conclusions regarding the EC case. For example, Carole Webb, points out that "the govern-

ments hold the gates between the Commission and their domestic politics," op. cit., p. 18. Similarly, Donald Puchala has stressed the important role of domestic politics as a factor behind EC policy achievements. See his "Domestic Politics and Regional Harmonization in the European Communities," World Politics, Vol. 27, No. 4 (July 1975) 496-520. Also see, Donald Puchala and Carl Lankowski, "The Politics of Fiscal Harmonization in the European Communities," Journal of Common Market Studies, Vol. 15, No. 3 (March 1977) 155-179.

18. The important role of national bureaucracies in pre- and post- decisional politics in the EC is stressed by Donald Puchala in his "Domestic Politics and Regional Harmonization in the European Communities," op. cit.

19. Robert Dickerman has pointed to the shorter distance between bureaucrats and political leaders in Scandinavia as compared to North America. He argues that this situation helps reduce anxiety by increasing the "confidence that political judgment rather than organizational judgment will determine national decisions." op. cit., p. 222. However, just as political awareness of administrative activity might be enhanced by the relatively small size of the Scandinavian decision-making machinery, the flow upward from the bureaucrats to the cabinet level might also have a greater impact on the thinking of the political leaders. In close working-teams of civil servants and politicians, it is difficult to ascertain who's perceptions, ideas, and objectives are finally reflected in the resulting policy decisions. So, the relatively shorter distance might not only help reduce anxiety but also contribute to a greater bureaucratic impact on national policy formulation.

20. Similar attempts at increased foreign ministry control have been noted in the EC as well; Carole Webb, op. cit., p. 26. Keohane and Nye argue that foreign ministries should encourage constructive transgovernmental contacts, and that attempts to cutting such contacts would be futile. op. cit., p. 242.

21. Keohane and Nye seem to imply a similar concern about preserving the familiar as a motive behind U.S.-Canadian collaboration; "in the 1970s the regime seems to have been restabilized on the basis of awareness of the potential joint losses from disrupting economic interdependence and acceptance of the important role of informal transgovernmental networks in managing relations." op. cit., p. 216.